THE COLLECTED WORKS
OF PAT LOWTHER

the COLLECTED WORKS of Pat Lowther

EDITED BY
CHRISTINE WIESENTHAL

NeWest Press

COPYRIGHT © CHRISTINE WIESENTHAL 2010

All rights reserved. The use of any part of this publication reproduced, transmitted in any form or by any means, electronic, mechanical, recording or otherwise, or stored in a retrieval system, without the prior consent of the publisher is an infringement of the copyright law. In the case of photocopying or other reprographic copying of the material, a licence must be obtained from Access Copyright before proceeding.

LIBRARY AND ARCHIVES CANADA CATALOGUING IN PUBLICATION

Lowther, Pat, 1935–1975
[Works]
The collected works of Pat Lowther / edited by Christine Wiesenthal.

New audio materials available via World Wide Web as a podcast.
Poems
Includes bibliographical references and index.
ISBN 978-1-897126-61-5

    I. Wiesenthal, Christine S. (Christine Susan), 1963–
    II. Title.
    III. Title: Works.

PS8573.O9A17 2010   C811'.54   C2009-906223-2

Editor for the Board: Douglas Barbour
Cover and interior design: Natalie Olsen, Kisscut Design
Photo of Pat Lowther: Peter Hulbert / Vancouver Sun

NeWest Press acknowledges the support of the Canada Council for the Arts, the Alberta Foundation for the Arts, and the Edmonton Arts Council for our publishing program. We also acknowledge the financial support of the Government of Canada through the Book Publishing Industry Development Program (BPIDP) and the Social Sciences and Humanities Research Council (SSHRC).

201, 8540–109 Street
Edmonton, Alberta T6G 1E6
780.432.9427

NeWest Press www.newestpress.com

No bison were harmed in the making of this book.
We are committed to protecting the environment and to the responsible use of natural resources. This book was printed on 100% post-consumer recycled paper.

1 2 3 4 5 13 12 11 10 printed and bound in Canada

IN MEMORY OF ARDEN TINMOUTH,
LORRAINE VERNON, AND FRED COGSWELL
& FOR PAMELA BANTING AND GAIL SOBAT

11	Acknowledgements
13	Introduction
25	A Note on the Text

27	**EARLY UNCOLLECTED AND UNPUBLISHED WORK** (1961–1967)
55	**THIS DIFFICULT FLOWRING** (1968)
97	**THE AGE OF THE BIRD** (1972)
103	**FROM *INFINITE MIRROR TRIP*** (1974)
113	**MILK STONE** (1974)
183	**A STONE DIARY** (1977)
253	**LATER UNCOLLECTED AND UNPUBLISHED WORK** (1968–1975)

319	Notes on the Poems
329	Index of Previously Unpublished Poems
330	Index of Previously Uncollected Poems
331	Index of Poem Titles

ACKNOWLEDGEMENTS

For permission to reprint copyrighted and previously unpublished material, I am grateful to the Estate of Pat Lowther: Alan Domphousse, Kathy Lyons, Beth Lowther, and Christine Lowther. Beth Lowther and her wonderful son, Rowan, deserve special thanks for their invariable patience and good cheer in accommodating my endless requests for access to the material. The work for this edition was made possible by a grant from the Social Sciences and Humanities Council of Canada.

    Digital preservation and storage of archive materials would not have happened without the help of Joyce Tam and her team from the former CRC Humanities Computing Studio at the University of Alberta. Gary Kelly and Patricia Demers provided valuable advice and support in the early stages of this project. Olivia Street proved as superb a reader and research assistant as I could ever hope to find; I am grateful for her efficient help with everything from reference materials to textual collation, typescript formatting, and much more. Special thanks to everyone at NeWest Press, especially Lou Morin, Tiffany Foster, Andrew Sharp, Deanna Hancock, Paul Matwychuk, Doug Barbour, and Natalie Olsen, for their enthusiastic belief in this work.

    Brad Bucknell contributed typically incisive insights to all aspects of this project, and also assisted generously in the process of digitizing Lowther's archive. Finally, Maureen Enns lent me a sanctuary: acres of glorious space and a studio with a view, in which I could finish this work in absolute comfort and creative peace.

    CSW, Ghost River, Alberta

INTRODUCTION

Writing is a kind of wrestling with the opacities of our own understanding, with the limits of the language we use. And like Jacob's wrestling with the angel, it is done to win a blessing.
PAT LOWTHER from an unpublished essay, "A Kind of Wrestling," ca. 1964–5.

Assembled here for the first time in the most comprehensive edition to date are the complete, published poetry collections of the late Pat Lowther, along with a generous selection of previously uncollected and unpublished works. Together, this body of work traces the development of one of the briefest but most compelling literary careers in modern Canadian poetry. As a high school drop-out in the post-war, working-class milieu of North Vancouver, Lowther, born Patricia Louise Tinmouth in 1935, began an unlikely literary apprenticeship that unfolded against the demands (and financial strains) of an early first marriage and early motherhood, both at age eighteen. In 1957, with her second child, Katharine, barely a year old, she enrolled in an adult-education creative writing class, and began submitting her poems, signed "Mrs. P. Domphousse," to contests aimed at amateur writers, sponsored by the Alberta chapter of the Canadian Authors Association. Her earliest publications also included regular appearances in *Full Tide*, the members-only organ of The Vancouver Poetry Society, a traditionalist literary club Lowther joined in 1962, apparently at the encouragement of Roy Lowther, the man who would become her second husband the following year. But Lowther's modest early aspirations and exposures as a writer broadened in reach considerably during the mid-sixties, due in no small part to her permanent relocation, with Roy, to Vancouver City, in 1963. There, introduced to writers such as Milton Acorn, Dorothy Livesay, Patrick Lane, bill bissett, and Lionel Kearns, Lowther tapped into more diverse artistic circles energized by the influences of feminism and postmodernism, the politics of the New Left and of counter-cultural youth movements. The upshot enabled her to cultivate a contemporary—and distinctly politicized—poetic voice and vision that were quick to reach both established and experimental literary magazines such as *The Fiddlehead, Prism, Ganglia,* and *blewointment*. It was a hard-won preliminary round of her "wrestling with the angel" that was also soon showcased in Lowther's 1968 debut collection, *This Difficult Flowring*.

Despite the additional responsibilities of a second young family to care for—daughters Beth and Christine joined Pat and Roy in swift, sisterly succession in 1966 and 1967—Pat Lowther made striking progress in her writing career after the appearance of *This Difficult Flowring*. To fast-forward a mere seven years is to underscore the extent of her achievements, for by the autumn of 1975, the former high school drop-out from the hinterlands of North Vancouver was hectically busy heading a national literary organization, The League of Canadian Poets, and teaching creative writing at the University of British Columbia. She had produced a second volume of poetry, *Milk Stone*, with the small press Borealis in 1974; one year later, she awaited the appearance of her third collection, *A Stone Diary*, with a major publisher, Oxford University Press. In the interim, she had also published a fine broadsheet folio, *The Age of the Bird* (1972) and had written and produced an innovative, critically acclaimed performance piece for Vancouver's MacMillan Planetarium, entitled *Infinite Mirror Trip: A Multi-Media Experience of the Universe* (1974). Lowther had, moreover, become a respected public voice not only as an artist and arts administrator, but as a political activist as well. A long-time socialist and supporter of the New Democratic Party, she was by 1975 newly appointed to British Columbia's Interim Arts Board under Premier David Barrett. Somehow, in the midst of this flurry of professional activity, and with her second marriage in dire turmoil, Lowther was also beginning to envision her next project, "a thing that is still in progress, called 'Time Capsule.'" [1]

The abrupt end of Pat Lowther's generously resourceful and creative life, by spousal homicide in September 1975, remains one of the sorriest events in our recent literary history.

As is the fate of most poets, all of Lowther's poetry collections have long since been out-of-print, including her best known, *A Stone Diary*, posthumously published in 1977 and remaindered by April 1981. (As is also the case with many poets, even today, much of her work was not easy to get a hold of even while it *was* still in print: *The Age of the Bird*, for example, was originally issued in a limited-edition print run of 150 signed copies. But distribution was an intractable problem for many small presses of the sixties and seventies, a fact of relevance to *This Difficult Flowring* and *Milk Stone*, as well.) But unlike the vast majority of notable poets, the notoriety of Lowther's violent death ensured a prolific afterlife of commemorative tribute, not to mention appropriation of the dead poet's memory in the service of various artistic and social causes. It was as a gesture of feminist solidarity that The League of Canadian Poets thus inaugurated the women's-only Pat Lowther Memorial Award in 1980, to cite only one such instance. According to critical claims insistently repeated over the decades, Lowther's "place" in Canadian literary history is thus both "secure" and "permanent." [2] But what is truly striking, and suggests the opposite, is that ongoing claims and debates about Lowther's "legacy" have occurred in the absence of an adequately comprehensive and reliable edition of her body of work. *Final Instructions* (1980), a posthumous collection of early and uncollected work, is necessarily supplementary in scope, but more importantly, also compromised by a range of factors that include missing and unreliable manuscript sources, as well as missing relevant biographical context for the material.[3] The more recent new and selected collection, *Time Capsule* (1997), has been valuable in re-establishing the visibility of Lowther's work for new generations, but it is also limited by its selected approach, diminished by textual errors, and somewhat confusing in the content and arrangement of its final section, titled, as is the volume itself, after Lowther's last and unfinished "Time Capsule" project. The Polestar edition is misleading in that only a few of Lowther's "Time Capsule" poems actually appear in the collection's final section, alongside earlier works entirely unrelated to that last project.

This edition, then, attempts to offer a more complete and accurate presentation of Pat Lowther's work from the time of her first publications in the early sixties to the time of her death. It brings together in one volume the contents of *This Difficult Flowring*, *The Age of the Bird*, *Milk Stone*, and *A Stone Diary*, also restoring to the latter the missing "City Slide/4," a poem for unknown reasons (perhaps space constraints?) omitted by Oxford University Press editors in 1977, but included in Lowther's typescript manuscript for the collection. The opening section of this edition, "Early Unpublished and Uncollected Work (1961–67)," includes a number of poems written during Lowther's early formalist period, as she moved through her association with the Vancouver Poetry Society (records indicate her membership spanned from 1962 to 1967, ending just prior to the appearance of *This Difficult Flowring*). Many of the previously unpublished and uncollected poems that appear here, such as "Pastorale," "A Moral Tale," "Ballad of a Carefully Bolstered Illusion," "School Children in Spring," "Echo," "After Rain," and "Haiku" originate from this period. Others, particularly those from the mid-decade on, were written concurrently with the work that would appear in 1968's *This Difficult Flowring*, but which Lowther probably left out of that volume because they did not fit its over-arching "domestic" theme. Several of these poems offer early explorations of voice and subject matter that anticipate Lowther's most accomplished later works. The previously unpublished narrative poem, "The Squatter," for example, articulates a nascent version of the inter-locking ecological and social concerns that would come to dominant the landscape of *A Stone Diary*. Likewise, early nature lyrics such as "Salt Wafers," "Creek Delta," "After A Day Canoeing," "Rocks in Copper-Bearing Water," and "Split Rock" provide clear intimations of Lowther's identification and fascination with the elemental, physical world in such later signature works as "A Stone Diary," "Notes from Furry Creek," and "Coast Range." Still others, such as the previously unpublished "Summer Sickness," strike the distinctively "alien" confessional, autobiographical voice Lowther would reiterate in later work such as "Kitchen Murder" and "Losing My Head."

Of the new material appearing in this edition is also the text from one of Lowther's most ambitious and (for its time) unusual projects, *Infinite Mirror Trip: A Multi-Media Experience of the Universe*. In the spring of 1972, Lowther had written to her friend Dorothy Livesay about a "starry idea," "a planetarium thing" for which she soon after was awarded the second Canada Council grant of her career. Elaborately collaborative and technical in its conception, the "experimental programme" of *Infinite Mirror Trip* signalled one of Lowther's first major forays into realms of both performance art and the sciences that most intrigued her, notably astrophysics and evolutionary cosmology. The show was based on an original script she produced, but also included original musical compositions, vocals, and the planetarium's special audio-visual effects, which Lowther ultimately pulled off with help from the MacMillan's technical producer, Michael Koziniak. All told, it took over two years for Lowther to mount the production, which eventually ran August 12–26, 1974. When it did, it disappointingly failed to attract enough of an audience to complete its fully scheduled run. But though a commercial flop, *Infinite Mirror Trip* was hailed by local media as a precedent-setting "artistic success": "the first use ... of the planetarium as a total art form."[4]

For a long time, I believed that the surviving records of Lowther's multi-media script were limited to a few notebook draft fragments and one incomplete rehearsal session audio tape. But when I returned in 2008 to the papers kept by Lowther's daughter, Beth, and re-examined the "Red College" notebook in which the draft "fragments" appeared—interspersed with drafts of many other unrelated poems destined for *Milk Stone* and *A Stone Diary*—I realized that the notebook contained a whole sequence of nineteen sections from the *Infinite Mirror Trip* script, untitled as such, but each numbered in the margins. These sections appear completely out-of-sequence in the notebook (which is typical of Lowther's composition habits), but the numbering enabled me to reconstruct the sequence which appears here. Whether these nineteen sections represent the complete and/or finalized draft of the show's script is another question; it is entirely possible that they don't. Nor can the text alone, obviously, replicate "the total art form" that was Lowther's original "multi-media" production. Nevertheless, as a window onto an ephemeral performance piece, one of the first such shows by a West Coast woman poet, the text is valuable, providing rich new insights into Lowther's cosmological exploration of the "relationship between inner and outer space," and her show's attempt to convey, in her own words, "the excitement and complexity of the natural world," as opposed to "current concerns with mysticism and the supernatural."[5]

The last section of this edition gathers together a selection of unpublished and uncollected work which Lowther produced from 1968 on, as she rapidly established a wider literary profile and reputation in the wake of her first book's appearance. Among the previously uncollected works reprinted here is an experimental essay, "The Face," which might also be described as a prose poem in three parts. Originally published in 1974, "The Face," like *Infinite Mirror Trip*, reinforces the role of science, science fiction, and new technologies in shaping Lowther's distinctive postmodern vision of a "wired" world in which human experience could be mediated, sublimated, and extended in unprecedentedly exciting—and frightening—ways. This growing preoccupation of her mature writing phase is also clearly evident in previously unpublished work such as "Stereoscopy: An Island," a revised version of a much earlier poem draft from the early sixties. Originally, Lowther's draft of this poem had been titled, simply, "The Island." As the revised title suggests, in re-working the poem, she chose emphatically to impose the technological onto the "natural" world, introducing the idea of the speaker's vision itself as the product of an optical device designed to enhance "the island" in three-dimensional relief and depth, against the "dark starry swell of sea"—an imaginative extension of the poem's concern with the effects of humans on the environment.

Of the poetry that Lowther was producing near the time of her death, the work-in-progress that she called "Time Capsule" has attracted special attention. During her last public reading in the summer of 1975, she described her vision of the project as "a complex kind of witness that maybe has been buried, or/and is dug up at some time in the future ... It starts out with a physical description of human beings.... And then it goes through some things ... like skin ... and ... the hands, 'agile pentacles,' and so on. And eventually, it gets into things like history, and context, and continuity."[6] The project Lowther alluded to here came to light again in the spring of 1977, during Roy Lowther's trial for murder. Attempting to portray himself as an aggrieved victim of an unfaithful wife, Roy had compiled copies of poems written by Pat (among others) which he felt proved her guilt, and his own public humiliation. Among these were "seven poems" from the "Time Capsule" project, including "Continuity."[7] Two decades later, it was the "Time Capsule" project that the editors of Polestar Press accentuated as the keynote of their new and selected edition, noting only that "new poems that comprise the *Time Capsule* section of this book were gathered from a manuscript that Lowther was working on at the time of her death, and which she had entitled *Time Capsule* [sic]. Some of the [other, unrelated] poems were gathered from notebooks and papers by her daughter Beth" (15).

While it was always possible to identify a handful of the "Time Capsule" poems from Pat's own descriptions and other records, an actual "manuscript" file of the project-in-progress did not appear to exist. At least, it was not until 2008, almost ten years after I began to work with Pat's archive, that I discovered a loose-leaf sheaf of typed poems that I had no record or recollection of having come across before. Headed "from TIME CAPSULE" and bearing Pat's signature on the lower right title page, the stack of fifteen poems is typed out on watermarked bond paper. It is (unfortunately) not paginated. As I then discovered, having once located this typescript, most of the poems from this "Time Capsule" project correspond to holograph drafts in a pale green notebook that was submitted as evidence in the court proceedings against Roy Lowther. To complicate matters more, the notebook is also interspersed with draft fragments from earlier of Pat's works, such as "Chacabuco, the Pit," and "The Sun in November," poems she had been working on by late fall of 1973. Although there is no indication in the notebook that any of the poems belong to a "Time Capsule" project, they are virtually identical to their typescript counterparts, which Lowther at some point assembled under that title. It is possible, then, that for her "new" "Time Capsule" project in 1975, she was going back to revive poems already completed in the recent past— in which case, her comments regarding a "complex kind of witness ... buried ... and dug up at some time in the future" also take on the intriguing valence of possibly referring to her own process of poetic recycling and recombining.

So perhaps it is not surprising that although they initially appear as diverse in content as they are in form, the "Time Capsule" poems that begin "with a physical description of human beings" actually foreground evolutionary and anthropological concerns with the "origin of the species" that one can clearly trace back to *A Stone Diary* and *Milk Stone*'s long poem, "In the Continent Behind My Eyes," not to mention even earlier incidental poems such as 1969's "Skin Over Pompeii"—a clear forerunner to "Time Capsule"'s "Imagine Their Generations." Readers will also note correspondences between such "Time Capsule" poems as "Their Hands," and the much earlier "A Chant of Hands"; or between "Time Capsule"'s "Context" and *A Stone Diary*'s "Nightmare," to single out only a few examples. Gauging from the poems that appear in the typescript and the notebook, moreover, the aim of Lowther's emergent project also seems recognizable, involving in this case radical juxtapositions of "context" and "history" designed to rattle such fundamental oppositions as past and present; "primitive" and "modern"; personal and cultural; consciousness and unconsciousness; vision and blindness of the eye/I. Despite the collision of time frames that occur among them, that is, the "Time Capsule" group of poems—even as an unfinished project—effectively underscore latent "continuities" between such oppositions. Each individual "clown's coat" of skin thus "mimics history" ("Skin"), while in "History," "another age / sifts down dry snow," or holds on, "impacted in rock": "holding on / holding / on holding." The apparently archaic tribe of "Their Mythology" celebrates a "passage to wakening" which is precisely what eludes the apparently contemporary, but oblivious, viewers of "Newsreel." The young Greeks singing in the midst of the suburban present, on "a quiet street" "in Vancouver," conjure "an ancient season" that also comments ironically on the dying (or already dead) relationship of a couple arguing "inside" one of the houses the seven singers unwittingly pass by. The domestic space of a "closet" opens into the mythic dream space of a Pandora's box, "infinite in length" and reaching "down to the roots of the earth," to all the "appalling hungers" and nightmare phantasms buried there, beneath children sleeping in their "small beds." And the "closet" of "Context" is an architectural version of "the strange grey planet" inside the human skull ("Cada Cabeza"), grey matter which continues to "carry" atavistic shapes of the "primitive" and archetypal past into the present: "In our skulls' fonts / we carry / huge intricate flowers; / serpents and butterflies / cats with shining pelts" ("Moving South"). The autobiographical import of such poems as "Context" and "Continuity"—works that indirectly but inescapably allude to Lowther's own personal domestic "history"—are thus more broadly framed and situated within the ensemble of "Time Capsule" poems, beginning with its impersonal, anthropological commentary on the human "biped" in "The Animal Per Se": "the creatures were unbelievably fragile."

Given her violently abbreviated life, the body of Pat Lowther's work is relatively small. But it is nevertheless an impressive literary achievement: impressive for the creative evolution it represents, as a triumph over the obstacles of poverty, sexism, and limited opportunities for formal education; impressive for its experimental scope and its remarkably alert, early engagement with many of the cultural issues and phenomena that have come to crest in the first years of this new century. Whether as a forerunner of Canadian women's performance poetry; as a humanist/postmodernist closely attuned to the possibilities and critical implications of science and technology; as an environmentalist committed to cultivating her own distinct body of eco-poetics; or as a leftist who stalwartly refused to divorce her aesthetic practice from the realms of social justice and ethics, Pat Lowther was quick to shape herself into one of the more provocative and intriguing voices of her time. The work collected here is nothing if not a testament to the determination with which she "wrestled" against "the angel," pushing at "opacities of understanding" and "the limits of language" itself.

....

Lowther's archive, privately held by her daughter, Beth, poses some significant difficulties for editors. No doubt in part due to the breakdown of her first marriage and the subsequent upheavals in Lowther's life, the boxes kept by Beth contain relatively little material from the period prior to Pat's marriage to Roy in 1963. The archive is not only partial and uncatalogued, but has been subject to its own disturbances: first, as the thoroughly rifled site of a criminal investigation, and subsequently, as it has passed through the possession of various family members and their own relocations. Both incomplete and somewhat unstable, the contents of Lowther's literary remains also make it difficult, if not impossible, to determine specific dates of composition for all of the works. The vast majority of Lowther's drafts, both handwritten and typed, are undated.

The organization of this edition is therefore chronological by date of publication, although where dates of composition (and/or dates of previous publication in little magazines) is certain, these are given in the end notes and annotations which correspond to the numbered sequence beside each of the 194 poems appearing here. In the case of previously unpublished material, it has often been possible to assign at least a periodic date from circumstantial textual and/or biographical evidence, and thus arrange the material accordingly. In certain instances, however, where the chronology of previously unpublished work is particularly ambiguous or obscure, I have also noted this in the end notes. This is particularly true of the order of the "Time Capsule" project poems at the end of the book (numbers 180–194). Since neither the notebook nor the unpaginated typescript is a reliable guide to sequence, I have had to refer mainly to Lowther's 1975 recorded description of the project in an attempt to approximate the arrangement of these poems in broad outline.

In the end, what Lowther so astutely said of writing—that it is "a kind of wrestling with the opacities of our own understanding"—holds equally true for the work of editing. Any and all errors are my own.

NOTES

1. PL, Prince Edward Island, 1975, audio tape recording (in the possession of Beth Lowther).

2. See for example Christopher Levenson, Untitled Rev. Of *A Stone Diary, Queen's Quarterly* 85 (1978): 352–54; Fred Candelaria and Dona Sturmanis, Editor's Introduction, *Final Instructions* (Vancouver: Orca Sound/West Coast Review, 1980); Rosemary Sullivan, "Pat Lowther," *The Oxford Companion to Canadian Literature*, Ed. 2nd Ed., William Toye (Toronto: OUP, 1983): 473–74, and 3rd Ed., 1997: 682–83; Hilda Thomas, "Pat Lowther," *Dictionary of Literary Biography*. Vol. 53. *Canadian Writers Since 1960: First Series*. Ed. W.H. New (Detroit: Gale Research, 1986): 278; Toby Brooks, *Pat Lowther's Continent: her Life and Works* (Charlottetown: Gynergy, 2000).

3. For a fuller discussion of the problems with extant Lowther source materials, see Christine Wiesenthal, *The Half-Lives of Pat Lowther* (Toronto: UTP, 2005): 100–08.

4. Susan Mertens, "Multimedia Without the Pain," *Vancouver Sun*, August 27, 1974: 29.

5. PL, quoted in Mertens, 29.

6. PL, Prince Edward Island, 1975, audio tape recording (in the possession of Beth Lowther).

7. Court of Appeal Trial Transcripts. *Her Majesty the Queen against Roy Armstrong Lowther*. Vancouver, BC Provincial Law Courts. 4: 524, 549.

A NOTE ON THE TEXT
The original first editions of *This Difficult Flowring, The Age of the Bird, Milk Stone,* and *A Stone Diary* have been used as copy-texts for the present edition. They have been reproduced without emendation except in the following (infrequently occurring) cases: i) where an apparent error or inconsistency has been checked against the existing manuscript, the manuscript version has been used; ii) where an incidental editorial change in punctuation or grammar obscures the sense of a line, the manuscript version has been silently restored.

Early
Uncollected
and
Unpublished
work

1961-1967

I   PASTORALE

All the years I remembered those fields,
The colour of washed grapes,
And the webby well
Whose water would make frogs of princes
(And that is the point.
The myths, like the living people,
Wear disguise of the plausible,
But that is the point—
To become amphibian,
Live in diverse levels, all innocent.)
There I played at modesty
Not with fig leaves
But with leaves of the grape,
The assertive, acid, green grape.
Velvet dust settled upon my hair.
All the years I have been angry
Remembering so much wasted on innocence.
And yet they will never break the silver fences
For firewood, for summer firewood.

2   A MORAL TALE

O once I found a wounded lark,
with wings too weak to fly.
I nursed him through the winter's dark,
then gave him back the sky.

I sent him forth on shining air,
his sweet, swift self to be.
He climbed the sky like a crystal stair—
but came straight back to me.

I have no bread to give him more;
his stillness makes me rage.
But still he croons outside my door,
and begs me for a cage.

3   BALLAD OF A CAREFULLY BOLSTERED ILLUSION

Oh, love can trick and love can lie
And kill the angel in the eye,
Seduce the virgin in the dell
And find a bed turned down in hell
And drink the nectar of the blood
And find the rhyme for clotted mud.
Then, knowing love can shrink to this,
How brave are we who dare to kiss!

4   SCHOOL CHILDREN IN SPRING

They sparkle up to amber air,
Their ice cream dresses and taffy hair,
Their hopscotch, skipping rope, run sheep run,
Their cheeks like apricots in the sun.
And here comes the boy from all the cartoons,
With pie-round face and glasses like moons.

They gulp the spring like a soda, I think,
But brew something stronger for me to drink.
What luxury, in this vintage year,
To taste these bubbles in May-bright beer!

5   ECHO

When sun stains grass
with long trees' shadows,
I go out
and fill my lungs with air
to send my call
along the space of street
to her, bike-riding,
back straight, Infanta of motion,
possessing the sectors of sunlight,
easy, alert joy
in her new skill —
   "Katharine"
   "Co - ming"
bell and bell-echo on the air.

6   AFTER RAIN

   The greyness has drained at last.
   Under the trees, the air gleams
   Like a sky-green glass.
   Like a fountain, opaque with bloom,
   The pear tree stands,
   Lifting its white plume;
   And in this blossoming it seems ·
   My heart puts forth green hands—
   Not to hold you, never to hold you fast—
   Only to touch you gently as you pass.

7   ON THE BRIDGES

   See them on all the bridges—the people waiting to fall, the
                               barbed-wire people.
   See them at clangorous corners, in bathrooms, on beaches.
   See them driving Ferraris or toying with razors,
   Avoiding mirrors or staring expectantly into them,
   The leapless, the unresolved, on all the bridges.

8   BIRDSONG

     What is the unthinking nature of birds—
     Swift knife-thrown flight, all business,
     Song without the applause of consciousness,
     This is the claim we feel most bitterly denied.
     In dreams we own air.
     Regal as migrant swans, we sail obedient winds.
     But man is a brittle perpendicular of bone
     Supporting a globe too heavy, too valued for flight,
     For that sweet uncomplexity—
     And song is a long tormenting tension in his throat
     And a heaviness of arms.

9   HAIKU

     April plucks my sleeve,
     offering fat fistfuls of
     red japonica.

10 I LIFT TO THE NOTES

I lift to the notes
Of a far flute,
A high white
In the dark of many voices.

I stood in a servant's posture,
And my hands were like
Five-pointed stars,
And my body was a shaft of light.
For this, to be quenched in darkness?

I shall cry out,
Over the crowd,
Over the roar of tides and years.
Surely your eyes will find me
And the ravening darkness
Shall not have me.

11   POETRY

Come walk with me:
I've laid this path
with mines
set to go off
at the first footfall
of perception.

Firebombs are in the mind
but so is love,
its soft flowering explosion,
scattering violent seed
sweet, sweet.

Such violence is
my work's intent.
Come walk with me.

Or if you fear
bring winter,
lay a crust of snow
to guard your senses'
frail autonomy

Armour yourself with ice;
no lesser shield will do.
I've tried your customed mail
of linked complacencies,
and know.

I practice
love and war
and you will not heed
your chill white smile,
your flag of truce.

But come,
The view is worth the danger.

12 CHOICE

      I have not watched the seasons by
this year,
         Not marked the months,
         Only I know it is late,
this morning,
         Late for the first injection
of light
         To be spreading under the sky's skin,
         And I am old, stone-old,
to hear
         This mounded earth muttering
unwelcome waking,
         And the thick spider-speech
of fruit trees
         Clotting the close horizon;
         And I wait for a hand
to stifle,
         As one would stifle a yawn,
         The faint exhalation of the city's
night-time neon.

      Then to turn away,
         Not to send out breath, stretched eyes,
and all senses,
         Nor wait for the first bird
to tongue the air,
         Not to be the clear scream and wingbeat
of sun
         Over everything piled and particularized
with frost,
         Not bear this chill integrity
into the day...
         But to turn, fleshy and small,
exact,

>   To the full noon's spectrum
>   And thousand alternatives
> demanding choice,
>   Demanding cultivation, and the stone years
> set behind
>   Like winter before the miracle
> of owning hands
>   And a mouth shaped for the colloquial,
>   And now take on these vivid,
> numbered years
>   And build a world within
> a world, human.

13   DIVISION

When our mouths have slid apart
from the last blurred kiss
and landed, quenched, in pillows,
he closes on a private agony
and sends his last thick thought from me.
O even lulled in billows
of warm-wave loving, I know this:
Flesh has not healed his scissored heart.

The spinning female thing that lives in me
and all night weaves a blunt, blind skin
over the day's ruptures and incisions,
needing only the grace of his assent,
tacit in flesh's sacrament,
lives not in him.
The total of his day's divisions,
a soft ripping, widens stealthily.

Then shall I mourn the whole
and silken sphere of me, a mate to this
bloodied rag and lace
of a heart that took my hand
in hot despair of love like a command,
and laid it on his wounded place?
Ah, I can only kiss
the sound, sweet body, and regret the soul.

14   THE SQUATTER

Goat-bearded clean old man
lives on the point
where the rocks are celled, windowed
skulls;
lives in a confiscated Japshack.

The speedboat people will tell you:
    the place has a forty-degree lean,
    only the vines hold it up,
    never known paint since the year one.

Older islanders could tell:
    the west window, from inside, 's a mosaic of grape-vine leaves,
    the room's full of peridot light sieved through leaves,
    the old man makes his tea in a small porcelain pot
    forgotten in that terrible abrupt
    exodus.

Bony hard-veined old man
sets his traps in the first light;
a wedged spike serves in place of one oarlock;
a jam tin for bailing.

The realty dealers will tell you:
    his place stinks of crab,
    he boils them outside in a cannibal kettle
    beside the well,
    but the well's good.

Long neighboured islanders could tell:
    the carcasses lime his garden,
    the salt soil yields sweet peas,
    cucumbers, corn,

>   his pumpkins make fierce jack-o-lanterns
>   for half the island children's
>   Halloweens.

Salty brown-toothed old man
lives with the tides and weathers;
watches the sea
and thinks.

The summer settlers will tell you:
>   he's some kind of religious
>   fanatic,
>   spouts about Noah
>   to anyone who'll listen.

The older, the seasoned, islanders listen.

Islanders know things they can not say:
>   *the shape of a whorled shell*
>   *on the skin of the inner hand;*
>   *how the flood of the highest tide*
>   *by moonlight night*
>   *floats something in the watcher too.*

They will not say what they know
of the old man
dreaming himself Noah
awash in oceans of light.
Nor what they dimly know,
islanded themselves in the same sea,
of the old man's brain,
tight in the tanned skull,
sucking year after year
sea light

like a great sponge,
its volutes luminous
with silt of light,
furred like moth velvet
with the sea's green light.

Tough-handed slow old man
mends intricate knots in fishnets;
sows his garden;
freaks himself for the tourists,
hiding his salt grin;

        Watches with cornered eyes
        the overnight A-frames
        encroaching;
        reads the horrible headlines,
        thinks of Noah;
        waits between death and Death
            and the subdividers.

15 BEFORE THE WRECKERS COME

Before the wreckers come,
Uproot the lily
From the hard angle of earth
By the house.
Crouch by the latticed understairs
Rubbish and neglect
(The sudden lightning
Of sun
On your back
Between the opening
And shutting
Of the March-blown clothesline,
Rise and fall of the swift light
Like blows.)
Here a lifetime's
Slimy soapsuds
Curdle the earth,
In this corner
Under the stairs,
But have not killed
The woodbugs
Nor the moths' pupae
Which brush your fingers
As you dig
For the round, rich root,
The lily root
Which has somehow, senselessly,
Not been killed either
But has grown every year
An astonished babyhood,
An eye-struck Easter.
Pack it among the photographs,
The silver polish,
And the last laundry

Which will not again
Lift and shutter
For the shattering sun.
Mark its container   :   X,
Two intersecting lines,
A lattice point
Of time
And the years' seasons.

Before the wreckers come,
Carry away
The lightning-bulb of sun.

16 SUMMER SICKNESS

Every summer faithful
as sun my hands
burned with their own heat
infrared in the blood
long sleeves and gloves
in the zenith of summer

total immersion at Horseshoe Bay
in two feet of water
fully clothed (how can you
fall in over your head
in two feet of water?
boys on the dock weak
sprawling with laughter)
the capsules to keep me
from burning to death
dragging me always under water
even on dry land
wading instead of walking

consciousness blinking off
like a negative strobe:
clutch at tables and chair backs
on the way down
the malignant hiss
of the drug in my head:
cat and mouse

sitting pale and clothed
among tanned bodies
I was more alien even
than they could guess:
my body at war with itself
its own juices
fighting for territory:
my hands burned like cities
movements of armies under the skin.

17 BETH

A human child
so lovely and so right
puts smiles in all my corners:
the bends of my elbows,
interstices of all my bones
are lotioned with pleasure

Until the child turns
on an inner spine of pain,
some nerve whip coil
I cannot know.
All is disharmony.
Her happy reaching symmetry
is all askew
and I can only cry,
What do you want?
What can I do?

18 LYDIA'S CHILDREN

"Whatever they are," someone says,
"they're beautiful children"
and I know they've been puzzling
over Lydia:
white negro? thinly diluted blood?
but cannot dismiss
her classic angled face,
her unquestionably negro husband,
and the little girls:
black hair, beige skin,
delicate profiles,
and Greggy, golden boy,
hair and skin a monotone
dark gold;
and I think
of their beginnings:
telegram from her parents
to a girl in love:
consider some less irrevocable
step   stop.
And the rabbi
sending her answer:
remember the nuremburg
laws   love.

"They're beautiful children,"
someone says, and eyes return
to the exotic family
suddenly in the midst
of all-average vacationers,
as if in a vegetable garden
some chance of wind
and magic pollen
grew a miracle tree
with graceful and rich fruit,

the sturdy, delicate girls,
the golden boy.

Somebody smiles self-consciously
at me, travelling with them,
no longer pale, medium,
ordinary canadian,
but someone to be seen whole,
and grateful
to be travelling with
pioneers.

19   SALT WAFERS

The sea proffers,
like wafers on a palm,
islands, tufted, many-shapen.
The sea, at full tide, calm,
stretched like an open
hand at day's end, offers
these, with the sun's last rays
lighting their crests,
cedar-furred, thin-soiled crusts,
salt to the least shale crumb.
Such rich salt on the tongue
is an organic praise.
Somewhere the senses lock
on tactile memory—
the original, pure salt lick,
the clear water at its flood—
'This do,' murmurs the blood
'in remembrance of me.'

20 CREEK DELTA

Now, rocks change character,
furred with flat green tongue-fuzz
and minute pimples of salt,
and I smell the breath of the sea
that has breathed
mouth to mouth with me
since my time began,
and that I know
as I know what my brain holds.
I am restored,
walking among sea-mud
and weed-expropriated rocks
to the stretching-away sea.

21 AFTER A DAY CANOEING

Close your eyes and see water
closing over water;
beneath your eyelids great cool weights
of water move, dispose themselves;
or see under webbings of light
the furred and musselled shallows
where we watch with paddles wary
for a scraping rise of shell.
Your skull like a sea shell
repeats the sea
Wind v-ing the water, swell of waves
touching the shore thin and lacy,
their solemn weight curled under.
This pebble-dragging sea washes
the membrane of your mind
as the tide, nudging
upward, reaches for your
water-closing-over-water sleep.

22   ROCKS IN COPPER-BEARING WATER

bruised,
washed with amber and rose
like reflected light ...

each rock
is an untranslatable
poem
that will never be said
being
a thing transcending
human speech
and any word
i say
modifies, therefore diminishes
and is a lie.

23   SPLIT ROCK

I am divided
like a cleft mountain,
and the push and weight and motion
of my life
sizzles through that gap,
and the I of me
that is monolith
that would speak a word
luminous and whole as
a rock
is apart from the I
that stands dazzled
before luminous rocks
that round all my perceptions
to a whole,
and the white unquiet water
falls and falls
between those cliffs.

24   SALAAL

The little plump fluted white bells,
hanging in strings and garlands,
as dainty as pampered girls,
will ripen to black furred berries
under their dark leaves.
I'm told you can make a living
on them then:
Pick them and sell them
for funeral wreaths.

25 ION

Strange, the need to be hung
hooked on
some other ambience...

Hi, little polar bee!

—Buzz off.
   This hive's as tight as silk.

You see that tree
with pale silver-paper leaves
hanging in clusters
like sleeping moths?

Sleep like a moth,
or spiral
in a falling dance.

no I think I am not
worth the pain   .
of the one-legged man turning
circles on his own axis.

But have you seen the chestnut
in full bud?
Positively indecent,
like a full-grown phallus
on a baby.

The bee has been
here, I tell myself.

26 A WATER CLOCK

It must have been that Adam crouched to drink
Before he sensed her there;
Stooped snuffling on the brink
Of slaking thirst,
Cupped his wet hands, and stopped, aware
Of woman in her heat,
Across the wind.
It must have been the first
Confusion, the first splitting off
That the amoeba dreamed toward—
That the warm woman on the wind,
And the cool water, rank and sweet,
Cupped ready for his rough
Mouth, pinned him in crucifixion, gripped
His instant arrow sense,
That had been mindless as the wind
Or the water that, ticking, dripped
Through his fingers' curved bowl.
Sense, and his warring wishes, poured
Into grooves that must be forced and split,
Atom from atom.

He who had been whole
As an amoeba, or an apple's perfect sphere,
Began his first disintegration, bit
Into the round, unbroken fruit of here
And now, and tense
Began, declensions, seconds, alternatives,
Peeling away, endlessly, never stopping,
Like the tick of water dropping
From his fingers to the trodden-under slime.
Man born of crossed purpose, Adam
Broke his bond with all the rest that lives—
That veined integrity, whole skin of innocence—
And looked into the water, mirror, time.

27 HISTORY LESSONS

1. A family legend:
   my great-uncle Johnny
   came back from the Klondike
   diamond-fingered,
                   pearl-pinned,
   gold in all his teeth.
   He never put hand to shovel,
   or panned a stream:
           he opened barber shops.

2. Eliza McCain,
   height five foot one,
   when the government ordered striking coal miners
   (and everyone else)
   off the streets of Nanaimo,
   threatened to thrash a six-foot militiaman
   with her umbrella
   or, if he still stood,
   to go home for her husband's horsewhip;
   until the poor fellow,
   fumbling his hat and rehearsing
   alternative explanations for his superior,
   let her pass
   with shopping list triumphant.

   Unfortunately, the stores were closed.

3. In 1945, in Japan,
   walking alone,
   a young Irish-blooded Canadian
   came to a hillside temple,
   saw in its delicate carvings
   swastikas twining around the door;
   smashed, with rifle and rock and muscle
   (stone chipping, lacquered wood splintering,
   gut-lovely sounds of destruction);

    till with the return of breath
    and binocular vision
    he saw the symbol
     as it was   really
        old   so old
    so much older than the thing he hated.

28 TO MILTON ACORN

I see you as a hand curled
around a growing thing,
sheltering;
no one's that strong, I know,
but such strengths grow—
if not in you,
in someone who
might grow into the world
you sing.

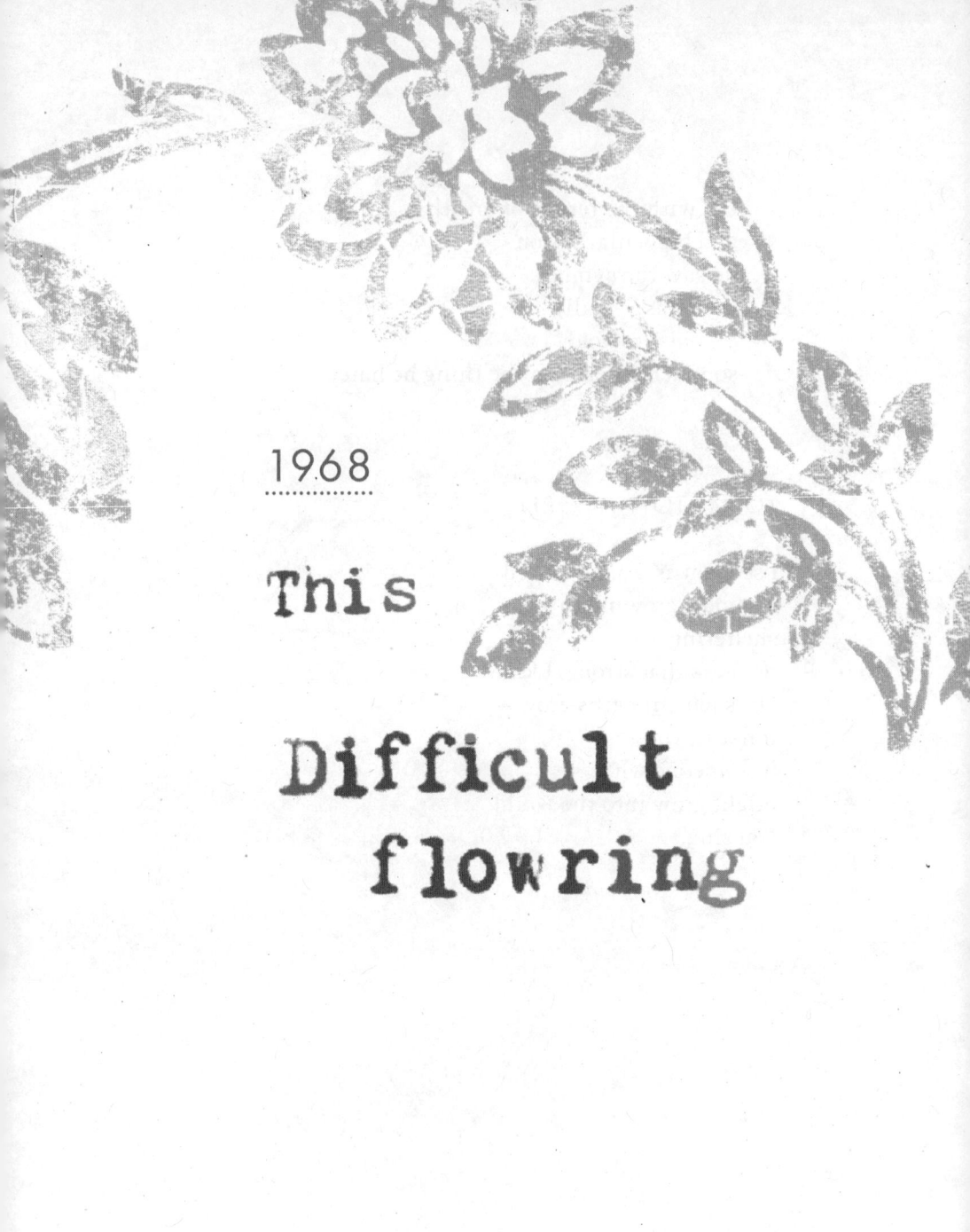

1968

This

Difficult
flowring

29   DAMN DOOM

Damn doom to
        day after day
           break our bright wishes
          on this work:
to carve a simple beauty
        out of chaos.
To make
        in this multi-motioned grid
          a lattice loop
            of space/time tamed
as air is tamed in a vase
        or a woven basket.

Best break the world
        like a wild horse
      or house
              the wind

30 MAY CHANT

May
and I squat in labour
crying the child Come down
Surely I am only
a partway-unwound
spiral of bloody cord
crying the child Come down
from his male cross
and the others the others
before him

Dionysus Come down
Osiris Come down
King of the kissing killing
Mistletoe
Come down

It is the men who come
tall singing
John Barleycorn is dead
but it was my child
my husband
they killed
and it is I
under the scalpeled earth
will cry
the good of his blood
and meat
Come down
to the root of things
and I who will
in the darkness of germination
stealthily gather
his scattered members
and bind them whole

31   LE ROY S'AVISERA

What sovereignty inheres
    or shall I cede
to this warm flesh rising
from the thicket of your thighs
    the scepter and orb of sex
    that you raise over me ?

        For if we fail
        the moment irrevocably past
        you burn
          with shame far hotter than
          your loving appetite
       commend yourself to study
       of my skin's desire only,
          shrinking before the troubling
          troubled mind.

Last night
we were afraid to talk.
You found a penny in the bed
and laid it on my lips.
    I have not yet deciphered
    what you meant.

32 PROMETHEUS

Prometheus
you've got to respect—
that business of the eagle and the liver
has a grand savagery
that commands consent.
But Prometheus with ants
up his pantlegs?
Or limping side streets
like an unasked whore?
(how do they know
with their cheesecloth eyes
her body is not
the most beautiful healing
they have despaired of?)

Or tune in on Prometheus
running hopping
juggling fire from hand to hand
sucking and blowing on his fingers.

You always said you'd puke this scene.
I dream you
holding out your palms,
two huge raw blisters.
I learn again
I love my friends too quietly.

33 REMEMBERING HOW

Remembering how
in the first luscious heat of sex
he was his own hothouse,
grew sensitivities
envied by all his friends,
his pen a green burdock
tickling the legs of passers-by,
implanting little barbs,
the seeds of private fantasies
(for every woman knows
a good man when she sees one,
he believed)

Now
that the juice is turned down somewhat
and mornings his root's a little numb
with frost
he still wears tongue on sleeve,
his pen's half-cocked
up every skirt
no matter how
unpromising

He feels
if only he can keep it up,
his hand
on some sumptuous ultimate knee
will impregnate
a whole culture.

34 ON READING A POEM WRITTEN IN ADOLESCENCE

Couldn't write then maybe
but how I could love —
When I said "Tree"
my skin grew rough as bark.
I almost remember how all the leaves
rushed shouting simmering
out of my veins.

Even now
I can almost remember
how many hands I had
hooked in the sky.

35 DIVINERS

Are we this — diviners,
Under our grey pearl
Smoke smeared
Sky,
Diviners of sun?

Look —
Where our hands join,
Water,
Green growth,
A townful of new babies,
A season of wine.

36   BELLY THOUGHTS

Laying my head against your body
is like listening at a sea shell,
the same echoes of fullness,
of liquid friction far inside,
the same feeling of holding
a whole world.

37   THEN

You will not know me then.
You will have screwed down your visor
against the least last grain
of gold corrupting pollen
on the air.
You will have freed yourself
of me
of us
of all the cursing hitting
loving world.
You will not even hear
if I should say goodbye.

38   WITH FERNS IN A BUCKET

with ferns in a bucket

with small shabby old

big nosed sleepy eyed

(ferns in a bucket) man

i shall go

where the streetcar tracks still unweeded

(surely there is a place)

streetcar tracks forgotten

rust in lees of rain

grey hat white hair

birds' egg speckled hands

(i shall go)

street lights fall dusk

first schooldays' dusk

surely there is

39 SPIN SPUN

    spin

        spun

            spiral tree

    apple tree

        lift hands

            drive you nails

of pink petals

            nails of honey

        into the wind's

            throat

40   THINNER THAN

>   Something thinner, more tenuous
>   than blood
>   (the branched
>   tree of the nerves
>   projected on a screen—
>   something like that)
>
>   connects
>   me with that drunk
>   blatting the words of my
>   unwritten poem
>   against the facing wall.
>
>   Like wires finer than blood
>   the hairs of my head
>   become alert;
>   I turn on him my blind
>   and secret eyes
>   but spy out only
>   the shape of his voice
>   moving
>   somewhere
>   among the branches.

41 THE COMPLICATED AIRFLOW

The complicated airflow in the house
stirred by my passing sets
the doors to opening and closing
one and then another
in an unknown order
like a pack of cards playing
its own solitaire.
The echoes fade like wooden etudes.
I think sometimes my passage
through this hall is like a falling
down a clef into the sea
and where I hit, a hissing
fault springs on the surface
(warp in a spider web,
spidering of a mirror

What is whiter than hurt water?
What is more flawed than a broken
stave of sound?

42 TWO BABIES IN TWO YEARS

Now am I one with those wide-wombed
mediterranean women
who pour forth litters of children,
mouthfuls of kisses and shrieks

their hands always wet and full
in motion

Each is the weaver of her province:
spinning a tight fuzzy world out
of her own body
and distracted mind

(a loose shred of thought
loops in "there is
the sun"
or "the sea with fish"
in the smeary congress of kitchens)

Now that the late summer stays,
the child hangs in
the webbing of my flesh

and last year's baby, poised
on the lip of the spinning
kitchen, bedroom,
vacuum, living
room, clings to the cord
of my skirt, afraid yet
of her first step.

43 BABY YOU TELL ME

Baby you tell me
to grow teeth in my cranium
and crunch down on
the gristliest parts of my brain
so as to make me more
digestible.

I say there are diners enough
with dear, sharp extensions
of their fingernails
manufactured for the purpose
with clubs ready to strike
at the pulse
of a hidden fontanel
(everybody's got a soft spot)
and teeth filed to approximate perfection.
I won't do your dirty work for you.

Anybody's going to eat me
he's going to know
he's had a meal.

44   MIDTERM EXAM

My white-skinned round-eyed face gleams
from the mirror new washed
    and my history
    professor says "Passed"
    and writes me a pass
    BEARER ENTITLED TO

              nothing more strenuous today
              than wrestling a bucking clothesline
              while wind blows
              my hair full of eyes
              for the beautiful
              salmonberry-yellow last time I looked   tree
              now black   peekaboo   seethrough   bare
              as the damned rain
              finally   for a while   stops

My body goes confidently about
performing its perfect right
of making milk before
the baby cries.
    It seems that history's
    given for my final mark
    a conditional pass,
    a little more work on
    the minor virtues
    (subdue hysteria,
    be reasonably stubborn)

              and I am assured of
              regular meals
              a domestic furnace
              time for occasional composition of
              a poem   a child
              protection from certain kinds of rain
              and therefore a probably natural death

The life expectancy of the average Canadian woman
is
     (white-skinned   round-eyed)

My white-skinned round-eyed baby
cries and is answered
at the first cry
                            Only, I wonder who draws
                            up the questions for her?

45   SEVEN PURGATIVE POEMS

I.   I watch the one I love
testing the tensile strength
of every day,
what weight of pain
it's sound to bear.

Go, man
ropewalk.
This day like every day
will take it.
I'll watch.
I'll watch!

II.   Spread out the morning
like a page
then ask yourself
what blot of blood
will rorschach
rampant
here today?

III.   The day will not come clean.
Blood will run down
our minds
before its end,
some clot coughed up
or vein slit,
the raw holes torn by teeth
will open
like dream sequences
a bloody darkness
in the day.

IV.   Piecemeal assassination
is a feast
for individual piranha
with pleasant faces,
friends, children,
and very
        commendable
                ideals.

V.   I am a spider
spinning bandage
out of my guts.
Some day
the roll will run
empty.

WHAT WILL I DO?

VI.   Poets are fat cats too,
fashionplate cynics,
alert
to the piss in the gutter,
the condom under the chair,
puffing their love
from needless-empty beds,
their grief
at convenient partings,
sleighting a dozen brilliant metaphors for phallus
none for guts.

VII.   Day's an Olympiad
of balancing
the beat and thrust of pain,
yet each night
besting pain
this bleeding love
comes fresh as flowers
to my flesh.

You dabblers in despair,
don't look so blank
when I'm left cold
by somebody's
forcefully phrased
boredom.

46   NOTES FROM A FAR SUBURB

I

Move your face now
  not in a wide motion
  but slightly, casually
    so the light runs like oil
      over the planes

    The others dance
  swift as electrons on a screen
but you
    you will allow me time
      to complete my thought

II

The man is a tree
        is a sun
is a burning-gasoline-haired wild weed
flinging   flinging
    GOD
            and
        melting matter

III

I am an eye in the forest,
jewelled and spittled
with dew
I am the underside of a leaf,
a bird moving
in my own brain

IV

In a far suburb
of the newest city
I unfold in a cool dim room.
Quiet I am Siva the lotus
opening in cool water.
Then you bring heat and pressure of flesh
and breath:

One of the many ways
the stems are
separate.

47   LEANING FROM CITY WINDOW

Leaning from city window
absorbing heavy October sunset, clouds apricot and wool,
leaning far out to grasp traffic lights, cars and substantial people
(a Diesel truck bruises my heart in passing)
leaning far out, far out, till the wind is an arm at my back,
is a paratrooper sergeant.   I'm out!
See how the pavement receives me, shatters me,
see all my life spread in glittering shards on the cool cement,
glittering fragments of traffic lights, of sunset reflect.
Now the girls from the factory grind me beneath their sharp heels.
I am a sparkle of powdered glass on the sidewalk,
a smear of frost.   Now a boy scuffs his toe and whirls me to air.
I am frost crystals, separate and dazzling.
I disseminate, claim all the city for my various estate.
Bidding myself farewell, I ride a stenographer's eyelash,
enter the open collar of a labourer's coat
and nest in the warm mat of hair at the base of his throat
and carousing above the street
ride like a carnival the wild loops of light in a neon sign.

48 ANGEL

That frowning angel toys with me, hides in the eddies of my mind,
   lurks beneath babble of bubble syllables,
   waits behind protozoan-chain of thought.
If I, riding a dolphin-joyous metaphor or clinging to swift shape
   of memory, shaft into darkness
   that monstrous angel rises
   sudden as a shark
   and spreads his arms before me.
He is beyond my governing and my evasions, he is a creature
   neither born nor spawned
   but grown like a coral,
   accretion of infinite lives and deaths
   into this sudden dumb integrity,
   this stark angelic incubus.

I have worked rites of exorcism against him, have made magic
   lattices, rings, pentagrams,
   have wished for a bubble of safety
   to carry me
   through food and bed and poetry.
I have performed the most potent exorcism, I have assimilated
   spring, freckled my skin with chlorophyll,
   opened my thighs to gold,
Have used my lover's sex for a divining rod to the very source
   of love which is like many waters
   flowing among intricate roots
   at the centre of the world.
And I have accepted all that love is, the ruthless hand
   in my guts, the rearranging,
   breaking and remaking,
   the flowing of myself
   in torturous dry channels
   over and through rocks;

And have not kept an essence of myself like a still walled pool
   that needs no renewal
Believing that such a still well could not nourish
   the terrible blood
   in its hard labour of changing stone to flower to bread.

And have not banished him, he rises out of someone else's poem,
   fits his face on the moon's dead face,
   mocks me in mirrors,
   speaks on a lost friend's voice.
O what cold fire is on his face! (I should have thought
   I burned and burned
   the sharp edge of my innocence
   to gentle ash).
His eyes are holes beyond which there are no horizons;
   they have not pigment, muscles, lids;
   they are organs of pure perception,
   ravenous, engulfing.

And those eyes tear the floating webs of words
   I have created;
   they break the delicate shells I have secreted,
   slowly, painfully,
   to house my loves.
And always, like Eden's fiery-sworded guard,
   he damns me for my sin
   of growing lids
   and muscled iris in my eyes
   and jeers me that my Eden was not this
   difficult flowring.

49 THE SLEEPING GYPSY

    I

Only under a sky so tender
  could mind invent
  the gentle lion

The nails of the man's
  feet and hands
  are twenty opals

Such hands work only music
  or magic conjuring
  of beasts

as blond and velvet as
  the bland lion
  lapping sky
    off the man's skin.

    II

The lost arm is asleep
  and wandering
  through worlds of dream
    menagerie

unharmed through quiet
  carnage moves
  the arm

to stroke an arching snake,
  a broken fawn,
  then on

to teach some screeching
  jungle bird a song
  one arm can manage
    on a mandolin.

50 AMPHIBIA

I

In air transparent
to our minds
as easy to lungs
we animate our city,
abacus of lights;
in interlocked conventions live
the long green life
of flesh entangled
as the roots of apple trees.
This is our element,
Our pavement only roofs it,
geometries pragmatic
as a bee's.
Secure in this
are the soft girl
praying 'World
happen to me',
the young man honed
to happen
to the World,
the woman, old,
her life run out
like the seasonal blood
or the milk from her breasts,
who fumbles
names of grandchildren
and lifts
pale cataracted eyes
to their tall above-her faces.

II

But like a death mask
beaten of thin gold
and jewel-encrusted,
there, that blinded face,
those blinded eyes
upthrust—
No, like a figured prow,
his profile
combs apart the waves
of outer air;
he moves
through living densities
our lungs would spurn.
Ions whirl
through his wrists
and thumb to wrist
he takes the measure of
the universe.
Strong in his element
he wrests
the tongue from rock
and measures time out
on a diamond clock;
then hooked by hunger
blurts into our orchards
and our dovetailed cities
gasping
fish-mouthed.

51   KILLER WHALE

The tamed killer whale
leaps for his fish
and falls back in a huge
angel of spray

Returning drops polish
the saddle of
immaculate angel-white
on his black pelt

When the trainer motions him back
he whistles and will not go
till he's ready

His eye through the magnifying glass
set into the pool,
his eye is serene, and unknowable
as the ultimate friend

52 THE EGG OF DEATH

      The thought of one's
   own death lies in a crypt of
mind, like a palmed egg, tight in-
tense seamless curve faint-ticking
time bomb taut with what we pa-
radoxically must call life. The
mind moves near it softly softly
not to jar it where it lies couched
in a hammock of blood in-
   holding its ripening be-
   gun before the womb.

     How can this be? — — —

that I move

        gloved   discreet
                    around my death
    when my neighbours'
casual hands
            devise the detonators

     for a swarm of deadly eggs
    and the explosions
of the shells   breaking
     through unripe cells
    release
       a flock
        of bloody
      black-winged
             birds - - -

53 TWO, SLEEPING

What do you dream
old woman
crumpled in sleep
like an empty corset
pillowed flaccid,
teeth in a glass,
what do you dream?
    'I dream
I'm a cradle again,
my moon belly
drawn taut with life
and my breasts slowly filling up
while I sleep.
I dream I am Mama,
plagued, nagging,
but Absolute
holder of absolute solace.
I dream that I suckle the world
and watch it grow fat around me.'

What do you dream
old man,
veined stick,
brittle ridgepole of the bed,
under sunken inelastic eyelids
what do you dream?
    'I dream
I am rector and rod,
right as Moses.
The law lives in my lifted hand.
My sons' eyes
whiten toward me,
they say 'Sir'.

The little girls court
my favour
bringing in shelled murmurs
their brothers' mischiefs
for my delicious wrath.
O I dream
I am master again
and when I draw in my breath
to speak
the world listens.'

54 IN PRAISE OF YOUTH

My father was a confirmed
lampshade-on-the-head man.

Legends are told
of his dancing,
his ukulele solos;
he could always be counted on to rise and declaim:

"It behooves me on this
    felicitous occasion..."

Now though he may rise
glass in hand,
to argue politics:
    "A pox on all your houses"
or instruct granchildren
in the art of showing off.

Gone are the grass skirts
the turned-out hats
the bundles of leeks behind the ears.

Man it makes me old
to see him fat and sixty
doing his drinking sitting down
while the lampshades
stay on the lamps.

55   A CHANT OF HANDS

Hands are beautiful things
grasping a hammer
or making bread
or moving passionately to say
what words stumble-toed run after

Hands are the organs of sex
calendars of experience

Hands touch where the impulse
of love will come
a breath later

Hands and the uses of hands
are beautiful things
How shall we not remember
the hands of our friends
with wine bottles and bread knives?

Hands have made
face-shaped wounds in my body
have made my hands move
in the shapes
of known beautiful voices

Hands are beautiful things
Wounds have entered all of us
where our hands have touched
tables beds handles of cups

The hand is quicker
than the mind
Hands pick up instruments
so that the mind may do
what the hands have already decided

Hands are themselves musicians
singers and dancers
architects
They impose judgement on what
imagination proposes
Hands have their own
kind of imagination

Hands yearn always
for smooth shapes
eggs olives
babies' heads

Hands are not afraid
of the rough bark of trees
or the rasp of unsmoothed metal
Hands are beautiful things

Hands want always to close
on whatever is
palpably good
to cup a whole peaceful valley
with fields and towns
and all of a dreamed
possible life

Hands are beautiful things
they want to dip into the blood
and hold the raw beating heart
they want to balance the sun
in their curved palms

O what we want
O what we really want
is to touch the fire
and not be burned

Hands know
what belongs to them
what intricate athletics
they may perform
what sudden spontaneous speech
they are capable of

Hands are beautiful things like trees
As trees change
the shape of the air around them
hands grow
into the world

Hands are beautiful things like rivers
Like rivers they move
and move the earth

THE INSIDER: A POEM FOR VOICES

He has rubbed his skin off
on wet walls
and regards
with still-born resentment
his peeled flesh
the color of walls.

His knees cradle his head
and his arms cradle his hips
and his hands cradle his ribs,
his arms are very long.

His excrement
is siphoned away
neatly without fuss
but his food
must be wrestled through
a thin slot in the wall
abrasive on his flayed flesh.

Sometimes an itch
provokes him
and his pale seed rises
through his hands,
a brief white stalagmite,
it too is siphoned away.

Sometimes, by osmosis,
he hears
far away out
a warm rough singing.

The sound is like childhood
or an animal tongue
lapping his ear.

Then he rubs his skin off
on wet walls
and regards
with stillborn resentment
his peeled flesh
the color of walls.

   * * *

A chanting of children: We gave him dandelion chains,
                                         lion chains,
                                         lion chains;
                              They broke and left their dark brown stains
                              that would not wash away.

                              We let him play our ancient games,
                                         ancient games,
                                         ancient games;
                              But would not let him know our names
                              or learn the rules of play.

A single voice: And who was to tell him
                      not to go drunken after daisies
                      and child's ring-roses?
                      Who would warn him
                      not to go drunken
                      after those faint scented
                      fleshless flowers?

With a small frown,
with an anxiety of love
and an iridescence of pain
like a dragonfly's wings
he went
squaretoed stubbing on skip-rocks
and clumps of grass,
hands net-shaped stretched ahead
after the butterfly-child-man-lover

A chorus of elders: Run, stumble-footed.
                      Hit, soft-fisted.
                      Hide with the hiders.
                      Hunt with the hunters.
                      Toughen your skin.
                      Please me, chameleon.
                      BE LIKE.
                      BE LIKE.
                      BE LIKE.
                      Love less.

The single voice: And his growth
                      was proliferation of green-stick bone,
                      irrhythmic spurting of growing
                      reaching into the rich
                      world, pruned
                      pruned always
                      the milky-bleeding scion
                      nipped to the scale
                      of a small garden.

And words gulped thickly
and the tentative art of lip-reading
the cipher of stance and phrase
and the mystery always mystery
of the ring dances
and the elusive rules of play
and the poison of luscious shadows
casual as a Pepsi-Cola
and even brief touches
of real bodies
And sometimes
an ampoule of light broke
in his mind
and spread,
funnelling into canyons,
shoving horizons
and lost itself
on barricades of soft 'do not'
and dried on the tall damn
BE LIKE.

A harmonic group: standardize, mechanize, homogenize,
Hup!
fraternize, synchronize, normalize,
Hup!
Did you hear about the farmer's daughter?
Yeah!
And the absent-minded professor? Yeah!
And the morphy and the pansy and the
Guy who listened to Bach? Yeah Yeah Yeah
(hehehehehehehehehehehehhehehehehe

A woman's voice: I am a woman; all that I might be
is like a cloud or mist in which I live.
Dragging my sex like a great dark sack with me,
I learned that this was all I had to give.
I brought to him my gift of female thighs,
my sex in a silken bowl of belly and hair;
he entered me with groans and hungry cries,
then washed himself as though I were a whore.
He'd read the pamphlets from the Board of Health
and knew that girls who give must be unclean,
yet knew of nothing else to choose from wealth
of all a giving woman might have been.
Now though I curse my sex, this heavy heat,
I will not give unless the giving's sweet.

The single voice: And the walls began to be builded
cell upon cell.
At times he seemed only wrapt
only a caul away
from the beautiful fearful
ambiguous, almost touching
him;
but their mouths
were centres of storms,
their motions were sources
of painful growing;
they threatened
and the walls grew.

A choir of learned doctors: The baby connects to the belly
                                         And the belly connects to the navelstring
                                         And the navelstring connects to the Omphalos
                                         And the Omphalos connects to the Om
                                         And the Om connects to the ego
                                         And the ego connects to the mother
                                       And the mother connects to the Oedipus
                                       And the Oedipus connects to the libido
                                       And the libido connects to the peer group
                                       O hear the word of Freud,
                                          etc.

Fragmented voices, speaking
  lines or shards of lines: O but we are guiltless
                                         Our charity extendeth even into
                                         the bat-hung caves of before night
                                         We nourish, we cleanse
                                         these dishevelled no ones
                                         That they rise not in our doorways
                                         That they emerge not from manholes
                                       in our paved streets
                                         Although some twig of us remember
                                       those darkage moondogs
                                       stark in their stink
                                       finding some random health in dirt....

The woman's voice: Why are we so afraid of touch?
                              : the pursed fingers dipping,
                              tapping the bloodstream;
                              women breaking like bread,
                              men become more than a blunt prong,

                    become a subtle needle
                    probing a cloudy vein
                    before-speech;
                    even the slow slide
                    forehead to forehead
                    of other than lovers.
                    Why is the shell more dear
                    than those rich minglings?

The single voice: Listen I listen and sing:
                    what will bread heal
                    or flowers
                    or a voice?
                    Only my animal singing
                    lips the lintel of his ear.

                    Listen I grow my song and self
                    huge and branching carelessly,
                    complex and infinitely casual.
                    Listen I only know
                    my body is warm
                    and my singing extends it,
                    my warm self grows
                    with my song.
                    I squat and sing
                    and grow easily outward.
                    Listen some day I may
                    grow to reach him,
                    may slide like the silk first serpent
                    into the coiled ear,
                    the first serpent
                    who hissed 'Be human'.

And maybe those clenched five-petalled palms
will uncurl partly,
enough for touch.
The rest will be up to you:
you must learn to be
the light-eyed snake in the dumb garden.
Study the serpent
who stretches in the spring
and sloughs the dead constricting skin
from eyelids,
breathing pores,
and all his parts;
who led us naked and confident
to all touch.

The

Age

of the Bird

1972

57   THE AGE OF THE BIRD

A laundry at Vallegrande
a windowless shed
tiled roof
in front two openings
separated only by a pillar

outside, a shirt slung
over a wire
a wheelbarrow empty
on scuffed ground

inside, the body
its eyes open
the head propped
in a tense posture

The souls of dead magicians
make our dreams

Dead man you didn't dream
deeply enough
you were not romantic

you didn't believe
legends matter
or languages,

a word for hunger
signifying nothing
compared to the belly's ache

Rivers swollen with malice
waiting to drown men,
the land falling away,
falling away from you
"mountains as beautiful as any
I ever saw in movies"

was it here a rifle could
sink into the earth
and grow
hard golden flowers?

The peasant base
has not yet been developed.
through planned terror
we can neutralize.
support will come later.

You should have put on
a mantle of mirrors.
you should have worn
gold and feathers
flashing upon
the tallest mountain

We have a new recruit:
a little female turkey
caught by Inti.

People of feathers
could you forgive him
for not wearing your scarlet hair,
for knowing no morning songs?

thousands of red banners
cheap cloth
with his face pressed on them
icons
have no need
for language

We are starting to learn Quechua.
interpreters here have,
or pretend to have,
little Spanish.
not one enlistment
has been obtained
and we have suffered losses.

Your father the sun
having set up a producing world
is no more concerned.
You think he would
wait a universe
for men and women
to step forth from rocks,
fountains, certain trees?
Not him, he knows how
to delegate responsibility

It is the age of the bird.

    Parrots
        doves
            small hawks

The hunters' hands are like birds
bloody with feathers
Your bones are hollow

from eating
small birds
A plane circles
The inhabitants have
to be hunted down
to be able to speak to them
for they are like
little animals.
the water is bitter.
an old woman with children
begins to scream
all your good wishes are confounded
the horses
will have to be eaten
the little soldiers
you sent back to camp
in their underpants
will return and kill you
your dearest companions
will fall like dead birds
Look at the stars.
That one
is in charge of
lions and jaguars and bears.

They have killed you with bullets
for that you were not
gold and silver
They have given away your life
for that you came in hair
and mud and giantflesh
They have cut off your fingers
for that you took
no attitude of prayer
before the male and female mountains

Far south they say at the time of death the heart
inside the body starts to grow
until a little man breaks out like a bird
breaking its shell; but he is unformed as clay
and weeps with hunger.
Then the wise ones of the tribe must feed and
cleanse him, shape his limbs, and then release him
to the high air where he lives forever.

       What happens to a soul
       abandoned
       in a laundry shed
       in Vallegrande?

       Or who is wise enough
       and bitter enough
       to loose this ghost
       in the wide sky?

       Sky dweller now
       extract the teeth
       of the cold south wind

       Deploy the guerrilla bands
       of lightning
       (so much better now
       for reconnaissance)

       Drop a few personal bombs
       on El Presidente
       and other aging movie stars

       Some day you'll be tamed,
       lured like a pretty visna
       to our cleaned hands.

       Not soon.

from
Infinite
Mirror
Trip

1974

58 FROM *INFINITE MIRROR TRIP:*
A MULTI-MEDIA EXPERIENCE OF THE UNIVERSE

I

[Lullaby]

Remember the darkness
the first curve
so easily sustained

Remember the curve
tightening   winding
falling imperceptibly in
heavy
heavy
The logic of that curve
heavy upon itself

crushing
curling
heavy
heavy

2

Has it happened?

What do you mean? Has what happened?

Are we outside yet?

No, it's exploded around us. We're still inside.

But how will we ever get outside? Is there
anything out there, out there?   [echo]

We'll never know.
Imagine yourself
a deep-sea fish,
a water breather.
At the limits of your sight
light breaks on broken water.
Those planes and breaking webs
of light mark off a universe's end.
We are like that,
closed in the splintered basin
of the first fire.
We are the universe made flesh.

Let the universe celebrate itself.

3

In the beginning the Word
one thick round syllable
the universe
maybe a cry so loud
we are still hearing its echoes,
a word shouted that shattered
the beginning, sent us scattering ...

a wrack of one's flying
a high outwind
dragging rainbows,
red rainbows of speed

racing apart with such terrifying velocity
flashing unrecognized signals
out of the ultimate cold,
cold

    4

In that desert between stars
the wind blows dust, dust
reddens our eyes,
dust in the lanes
of the galaxies,
dust of ice
in the cold desert,
needles of ice dust
or flakes of glass
or it may be
miniature door knobs
twirling
to the precise shape
of the magnetic wind

[Other Voice:] Is somebody at the door?

    5

The rub of the dark
against the dark
The white glyph rubbed
into the light
Rorschach of light whirled
spit, oyster-spittled

out of the webbed and layered whorls
gobs of nebulae

A blindness of galaxies
hoary hair of stars
such LIGHT to lash
these breathing windows

6

OH SO MUCH LIGHT

oh so much light

pinwheels and serpentines
windmills and whirligigs
sparklers and all-day
all-eternity suckers of light
such glorious toys
to please an infant god

7

The stars fall out
like petals shaken
or like fruit
in their generation
stars and the seeds of stars

8

They keep graphing
our history a molecule thick
on the earth's crust.
We begin to see
ourselves precipitous

as Keystone Kops,
more — brief as
subliminal commercials
shrinking to streaks
of light on film.

Centre us more
comfortably in time:
There are stars
that do not live
long enough for part of them
to become people.

9

Through one eye
I see a web,
precise filigree of electrons.
Through one eye
I see a cloud,
a shapeless puff of winter breath.
How strange to see
two faces in one mirror.

10

Cinder star
smaller than worlds
heavier than clusters
heavier
heavier
drawing in all your weight
to darkness
drawing in space itself
to a dark vortex

    danger   danger   danger

11

THE UNIVERSE INSISTS

upon order.
No star husked of light
stripped of its
delicate busy parts
nothing so heavy
so sucking, shrinking
will be allowed
to remain.

12

Are there star ghosts
trailing their wispy spirits
through emptiness?
Do you feel that gossamer
on your eyelids?

13

Meanwhile back in the nursery

For a star to be born
There must be mutual attraction.
There must be intimate relations
between excited particles.
There must be a rise
in temperature, a definite glow

Is it love   love   love
that makes the universe go round?

and around and around and around

14

This egg, golden,
multiple-yolked,
it turns, it turns.
Its clots of substance
achieve balance
They gather light
They press light to stone,
to earth, to water

This golden egg
it turns:
from it will rise
all creatures
singing and crying out

15

Light has shaped itself
into this mechanism,
all parts meticulous,
functional,
elegant as a music box;
even the jewel precision
of moons —
the universe itself
has a touch of whimsy

16

Stone of water
stone of green
sap and salt
first seen
Remember remember
who we are
children
of a minor star

17

And the whiptongue of lightning
first woke life
nor was it gentler weather
grew the hard and soft
the leafed and armoured
and the thinking star-stuff
that conceived the universe
A tree of life
whose branches lace through heaven
where we half-believe
someday we'll pick the planets
like ripe peaches

18

Can we really go out there?
Can we discover other worlds?

We can only rediscover.
We can go no where we haven't been.
The farthest galaxy in time's sight—
look, it's fine-spun as a baby's hair.

19

turn, turn, turn, turn

There is a wheel
that turns forever,
a wheel of flesh
a wheel of fire
A wheel of stars
turns in my fingers
A wheel of flowers

in the sky—

Milk Stone

1974

59   HOW CAN I BEGIN

How can I begin?
So many skins
of silence upon me
Not that they blunt me,
but I have become
accustomed to
walking like a pregnant woman
carrying something
alive yet remote.
My thoughts,
though less articulate
than image,
still have in them
something like a skeleton,
a durable beginning
waiting for
unpredicted flesh
and deliverance.
I would ask
you: learn as I learn
patience with mine
and your own silence.

60 WOMAN ON/AGAINST SNOW

Figure without landscape,
white with the many names of snow,
she makes her house
of skin and snow.
Alone
for the others are dead,
she is a small Arctic sun
curving space around her.
This world swirls,
changes with every wind.
She must shape the world
by being alive.

"It is scarcely possible to conceive
that a person in her forlorn situation
could be so composed
as to be capable of
contriving or executing
any thing that was not absolutely necessary
to her existence"

Necessity:
The Bone is
The Flesh is
The Outside is
The World is and
The Idea of the world is
The Idea of being human is
Hunger
and responsibility
The first/last human is
poet
shaman

   debater
       with the universe

                Give me a bone for my hunger
                Nuliajuk
                I will turn it in my hand
                till it speaks
                I will call from it
                shapes, faces,
                with my ulo
                I will call from it
                your creatures Nuliajuk
                I too castaway
                I mother
                midwife
                in the absence of the people
                I speak with the world

Give me blood for my hunger
Nuliajuk
when I have drunk
I will save a little
a thought will come to me
to help my clothing be beautiful
in the absence of people
I speak with the world

                At times the wind is elsewhere,
                no snow falls,
                the sky's lights crackle and hiss.
                Lost as the sun
                among all stars,
                she hears the whole night
                name her,
                Small Small
                Here-by-chance
                Belonging-nowhere-meaning-nothing.

                    She says stubbornly nothing
                    but poems come from her hands:
                    she finds food.

As Nuliajuk's severed fingers
came to life
took shapes and senses
the woman's hands
leather and bone
brown patient angels
work ritual

            Song arranges itself
            at the door
            of one's mouth
            One is abraded by grief
            like snow with many teeth
            The walls drip water
            and glaze
            Words name the dead
            For a time breathing song
            one is not alone

The white world circles
blank as a zero.
In the centre of white
a dark speck, living.
She is the pupil of that eye.

            Being-alone has been
            a name for death.
            Being alone when light fails
            and the traps are empty,
            she will sit crouched
            in her body
            and her hands stiffen
            still working.

61 STRING-FIGURE MAN OUTSIDE THE DOOR

Didn't I too catch the sun
in a cradle spun
of my own gut strung?
If now outside my house some thing
makes a sound like dry skins scraping,
should my bones dissolve to jelly
in my narrowing flesh?
It is fitting to strangle me in the mesh
of my own making.
I who made the sun
come in my belly.
I shall open my door
and accept the evil as I did before
the shining One.

62 IN THE CONTINENT BEHIND MY EYES

I

In the continent behind my eyes
voices are
pretending to be birds
They fly from rise to rise
of land
like a chain of torches

* * *

The city like an open brain
zaps messages
lights   avenues
A hillside suburb
lights up like a bloc
of dogma memorized

The first lamp post is
  a block away
    the next is half a block
      and then a quarter
        then closer faster
          mene mene pencil strokes
        how fast can you
          run runrun run

* * *

Hung between backyard earth and moon
I sway
like some elastic tidal creature
Stalagmites form
on the crown of my head
my feet grow trailing weed

In the continent behind my eyes
forms are moving

out of a funnel of twilight
Distance has blurred their features,
leaf mouths and silver fur
hands, postures of hunters
and gatherers of words

* * *

It is as if we grew
the city like a concrete flower
that we bear
on our spinal stems
and its seasons grow longer
closer together

until like us it casts
its seeds all year
love without death
demanding death

*The thunder lizard
lurching in a quake of air
loosed the first green white bract
that fell between his toes,
and pollen flashed across
the grain of sunlight,
a constellation
which he did not see.*

*Now all the barbed and winged
and honey-fleshed
inventory of seed,
sun's coin deferred,
keeps the blood warm.
They learned, who trembled*

*in the roots of time,
such flour and herbs
could feed infinity.*

*A petal's weight brought down
your world, old Rex,
and grew this furled and ruffled
flower in my head.*

*A photon's weight,
a deflection of light
across a jelly
was it?   invited us
out of our bodies
to make a world web in time,
to build on the rock Death*

* * *

The metronome of ice and sun
still ticks
where the blood ticks
in all the intimate corners

To find what I lost
at the exit of the forest,
lost in the beat of sun
and the light-maze of voices

I must go back
cast bones on snow
reread my first boc
before morning

* * *

*The cold like a stone hand
tensed so we could hear its tendons cracking
closed on us
That was a country we learned:
The palmistry of snow,
canyons between ice fingers
where the animals kept fire
under their skins.*

*We scavenged the bitter trees
for throwing-sticks
worked ice and bone and flesh
all winter
and Greatbrother Bear,
his huge soft teeth
paining him,
slept and slept.*

* * *

Here by the sea
a fluted woman
with a spine like music
unwinds a monument to water
while under the surface
hands hands hands
shape every gesture

I turn like a hand
with the curved plates of fingernails
buffing outward

as if a laying on of hands
could wring from stone
a pure dew to drink

through the scalp's pores
For I have bowed to stone
since my great brother is dead
who feasted me after hunger,
who taught me art
and adoration

* * *

In the white
country behind my eyes
a shape turns
with an unbearable weight
crushing his jaws
He too cries
like a bird or a memory

* * *

I break an island into crumbs
and eat it,
crunching salt between my teeth

II

Skin from me colour
and irrelevant sound
White as silence I walk
and can not determine my size
If I am large
enough to contain the universe
in a pattern of cells
still sometime I must scrape my knees
on ice-heaved ground
and bark
with an unused throat

Scattered around me are silver
shells of snakes,
out of place in this cold country.
I think they are shrunk
skins cast by the moon
in unguessed transformations

I pass an old woman
making a stringed instrument
with her back to the sun

I pass a young man
with two birds in his hands,
holding their fluttering against him.
He cannot yet free a hand
to act

* * *

The ice forest grows
like a speeded film of stalagmites forming
While I watch, antlered trees
fur a whole ridge

The sun stands still
in a ring of frozen trumpets

bringing my turned love
to milk stone
or build a tower from my throat
Tension between
notes spoken and words sung
makes visible
a structural shimmer
standing as long as my throat
can hold pain

Star-shaped I
build my cathedral
of this stone ice
from my left hand
trees and branching coral
from my right side cliffs
from the centre of my forehead
distances and curved horizons

* * *

The polar grid of light
harrows my brain
long furrows like
the bear's claws left

* * *

I wanted the wind to hone me
into a blade of glass
that would sing when tapped
but my shape is enforced
by the memory
of running water

III

When I was a child
my father worked with water,
adjusting flow and level,
going out from his bed
into 3 in the morning storms
to keep the screens clear
And once he took me to Rice Lake
where no one is allowed—
the water was flat as pavement

papered with fallen leaves
and flat wooden walkways
and there I walked on water

At the stem end
of the world I am
walking on a shell
of ice over water

I too am porous as a coral
city enclosing water

At some point in every journey
by purpose or unawares
one arrives at a rag edge of water

In this huge bowl my head
shavings of light
from patterned stars angle
off ice and smoothed stone
All space creaks
a sphere of ringing sound

* * *

There is a hole
in the world's eyeball
I jerk my foot back
from the shredded edge

the sea I had forgotten
to account for
the first metaphor

its endless business
Even now the sea is inventing

sex and death
spice it filters out like salt

I am always aware of
the origin of birds, he said,
their scaly reptilian claws
Yet I grew doting fond
of a little creature
in a cage chirping

*In the dance one hand
fits into another's
like the secret five bones
in a seal's glove.*

*Birds circled us
animals looked over our shoulders
the sun and the moon
ceased to bring forth children
their light was upon us
like clothing*

*One of us sang
with a throat grown
thick and furry
The great one said, Eat*

Is it that the web of the world
broke when he died
and left me this plucked end?
That we danced the whole world
into tatters with our first god
broken among us—
or have I stumbled nauseated
through millennia

sickened by something I ate,
the brain of the great soft bear
who wanted only to be left alone

*He was more beautiful even
than need made him,
as fire in the evening
or a bush bright with wet berries,
he was desire filled
and the belly warm*

*As he moved
so would stone mountains move
swaying to the edge of balance
and return
His steps made a trembling
in the dwelling places*

*In pleasure or hunger
his voice was like rough curling water
In anger he was the world storm
and his mouth a fanged cave
to fall into*

*Small against him with love
we charmed our weapons
we coloured ourselves
in his honour*

*One of us he took
under his claws
We could not grudge him
And afterward
we carried his great head
to the dancing ground
before eating*

* * *

From the ends of our fingers
from our mouths
before and after eating
the city began

It is throwing a voice.
It is killing an animal
without praying.
It is melting a mountain range
into a mirror.

* * *

In the spring water seemed
full of voices
whose words we had forgotten
We gave each other names
We found the cave he died in
Water ran down the wall
We gathered in the stench
of divinity
and washed ourselves

See how I strip from
hair, from hoarse innocence
to frail
breaker of covenants,
how like a pool in afternoon

I create every
possible existence
while behind me night
erases beginnings.

* * *

My fingers trace
his gouges on the wall.
Soon I will take a sharp stick
and begin

63 THE ORIGIN OF THE UNIVERSE

Laugh, or spit.
They have postulated microbes
building cities on a mucous membrane,
or a great sucking pump
like the animal heart.

I prefer laughter
visible
as in absolute cold,
or a boy working up his juices
for the ultimate
all-time champion
distance spit.

64 THERE WERE GIANTS IN THE EARTH

For Nutcracker Man
a thighbone was a morsel;
his teeth were precision made
to slit the kernels
of marrow cells.
His woman had long teats—
even so, the babies hurt her.
They never learned
to kiss, being content with
the delicate erotica of sniff:
they were simple souls.

The Nutcracker Man
the little people at his boundaries
moved like a blur
across his vision.
Their voices chittered to
a sonic whine,
no more significant to him
than bees buzzing

For him trees grew
at the rate of his digestion;
a generation of pygmies
could die in his sleep.
He kept his head low
to ease the weight—
his glacial motions
frightened killers from their prey
that he could eat.

Slower and slower he grew
in age; he accepted
without the need to invent it
the concept of eternity,
and saw only as jerky shadows
the subtle pygmies
bearing away his life.

65   VISIT TO OLYMPUS

Just 30 minutes off the highway,
past "Private Road" and "Trespassing Forbidden,"
up 3 or 4 miles of bone-aching gravel
(one place I chickened out
got out and walked
where mossy logs shored up the road
over 2000 feet of air).
About a half mile from the top
we passed the mills,
great toothless airy tombs;
we couldn't see how fine they ground
(the stones were gone)
but the Presences were strong.

The townsite was dead of course
as we'd expected.
Trees grew through the bleachers
by the swimming pool.
Buildings were half-demolished
(as though the wrecking crew
couldn't get paid
and left the job unfinished).

And walking softly
into the main temple
careful where beams were torn away
we found in an anteroom
an autumn-fall of relics:
old invoices and social notes:
> *Mysteries Tuesday at 8:00*
> *all those concerned please note ...*
> *New wine-tasting ... Bacchus invites ...*
> *Maternity shower for Danae ...*

It would all have been disappointing
except for the clouds

being so near,
beginning inches overhead
so that up there even a tall man
would walk like Jove
with beard and lion-locks of cloud,
in the cool seasons.

66   ARCTIC CARVING

They say it's country of dream:
so few go there

a cold place inside us
the body can't convert

There light falls in separate flakes
into the world mesh
Creation of all things
spreads outward

And there a man who had
never seen trees
was visited by trees of ivory
shaping themselves against his knife

No leaves suggested themselves
only rudiments of branching

only the blunt pure shapes
essence of trees
where like the mind at point zero
a white bird rested

67 VISION

The woman looks out of the whale's bone
her eyes eroded
sinking
into the marrow
the source of vision.
The whale cutting
the water
sings like a huge machine.
all his bones
have eyes.

68 STONE DEAF

Imagine it —
tympanum, cochlea,
cunning little frogs-legs ossicles,
all that delicate absurd machinery
petrified, rattling stonily
in the skull's cavity
like garnets in a hollow rock.

Or like a whale's eardrum
I saw once preserved,
blank as a great flint chip
and lonely as one cymbal.

And the blood's surf beating
then always like the sea
unheard on solitary stone.

69   PERIODICITY

Fragments of shell
shards of a protein alphabet

my hands are blind

at my skin's circumference
i fumble
seams   openings
(is this an organ
for breaking shells?)

i smell snow on this beach
what colour
are my eyes?

70 'AT THE LAST JUDGEMENT WE SHALL ALL BE TREES'
MARGARET ATWOOD

Trees are
in their roots and branches,
their intricacies,
what we are

ambassadors between the land
and high air
setting a breathing shape
against the sky
as you and I do

the spring also breaks blossoms
like bread
into our hands
as the tree works
light into bread

its thousands of tongues
tasting the weather
as we taste the electric
weather of each other

Trees moving against the air
diagram what is
most alive in us

like breath misting and clearing
on a mirror
we mutually breathe

71   NOW

    Now now I slide under from me
    into the water
    and its continents

    my foot does not understand
    geo-metry
    though I stand caliper-legd
    on land and water,
    but like a hand or tongue
    discovers doubleness

    and now as I slide under
    toes   palm   heel,
    my lungs take water
    my bubbles of breath become islands,
    an archipelago
    bright as apples

72 TOUCH HOME

My daughter, a statistic
in a population explosion
exploded
                popped
out of my body like a cork.

The doctors called for oxygen,
the birth too sudden, violent,
the child seemed pale

But my daughter lay
in perfect tranquility
touching   the new air
        with her
   elegant   hands.

73 WOMAN

I

I think I wanted to be
wings, the essence of wings
or a universal symbiote

As a child I climbed trees
and sang in the branches.
Feathers grew like leaves,

levitation became possible
An upwind under the leaves
lifted me like a rising song

The lightline of horizon
funneled into my eyes,
expanded again inside,

splitting my mind like a robin's egg.
Cracked but still singing I
took possession of the sky

Just past the first star
I grew aware of my blood
in its closed veins, a closed system.

Symbiosis had failed.
I was lonely as god
before the invention of colour

Space cold and pure
encapsulated me,
a virus in the universe.

II

Knowledge coarsened my flesh
I grew heavy
stumbling down endless flights of stairs

At landfall I clawed
in fear of air I'd marked
with curlicues of flight

Earth and salt sea
rocked between the two
poles of my knees

an omen, for I shrank
into my body and beyond
into the warm thick cave of genesis.

Remembering lonely sky I became a slave

to the whimpering womb,
that hollow mouth that never says Enough
until too late.

III

Shrunken between walls
I think of electric storms
in a bird's brain

I think of a tree
as a slow paradigm
for an explosion

There is still a delicate network of cracks
like a tree's branches
behind my eyes

resembling lightning also.
Some day you will find
feathers and blood
on the inside of the window.

74 THE LAST ROOM

I am waiting for you
in the lowest room beneath the building

I am smooth as a gourd
without resistance
my shape spreads
        downward
                seeking the lowest
centre of gravity

I spend hours memorizing
the labyrinth
        beneath our skins
                by which I came

waiting for your long shadow
in the passage

I am green as a gourd
but inside I am red

All through the folded hours
I am burning
        quietly

I am becoming a red hollow
skin
        a gourd for drinking

Only now do I recognize
shards patterning the dust
between my legs

they are my former skins

How many times
have I come here

How long have I been waiting

75   WANTING

Wanting
to be broken
utterly
split apart with a mighty tearing
like an apple broken
to unfold
the delicate open veined petal pattern
inside the fruit

I am arrogant
knowing
what I can do
for a man

I am arrogant
for fear
I may be broken
utterly open
and he not see
the flower shape of me

76 PSYCHE

I am forbidden

At the consuming moment
I am forbidden
to look

I am driven to
furtive research:

are there photographs

impressions on a pillow

a lost hair, a fingerprint?

My hands would be eyes
if I were less afraid

knowledge would devour me

Even secretly
I could not look
without trembling

without that hot

drop falling

on an unknown surface
of your skin

77 DEMONS

It's a kind of justice
for our having left them
face down
while we grew branched
metaphysics

They held out
dumb paws for grace
We gave them ritual

Even the spare comfort
they negotiated
we fattened on,
driving them always
to the edges

It's a kind of justice
that in certain seasons
they possess us
like planets,
like territories

78   THE PIERCING

You will be beautiful now
as woman should be.
You will move your long neck
and jewels will sway.
As woman should be
a pure chemical
breaking the bland compound
of conversation,
you will turn your head
and sever light
into its elements.
Men will drink
pure red and indigo
from your throat.
Now you are truly woman
said the middle-aged jeweller,
plunging the needle through.

79 BURNING IRIS 1

elegant man
in your wellkept body
and tidy clothes
give a thought to
the ragbag broad
smoking in doorways

doesn't the heat of me
reach like curling air
to your belly?

stumblebum iris
burning under revolving neon
blue as an iceberg
green as a bruise
see how she sags
through the spectrum

is it the turning light
or your sudden eyes
moves me through amber
to red as a hot stove?
here's where i begin to melt
to lose my shape
I need hands to squeeze me

crazy iris in her goodwill skin
thinks she can be
whatever shape you want
she'll have to buy new breasts
new knees and feet

but i'll still move it
like iris in pollen time
a touch can do it

that's what she thinks
but a calculated touch
sets her burning like a building
outside in the coloured street

80   BURNING IRIS 2

My neighbour is burning
the dead blossoms;
faded to vellum paper
they crisp in the fire
and now release
their last writhings
of fragrance, the crushed
purple, the grape wine tang.

All up and down
the lane, people
are biting
imaginary earlobes,
closing their eyes
as if in pain.

Surely there must
be a law
against burning iris,
sending the acrid
aphrodisiac
of dead flowers into
the neighbours' air

81   BURNING IRIS 3

                round   blue
       musculature meticulously
    fitted   almost   like   breathing
    they   relax,   draw   back   into
softness   to   let   light   in
their heat   touches   my   skin
like a hand   moving this
  close   they   make me   cross—
    eyed,   i am dizzy   on the
      round   paths   of
            blue irises

82 PENELOPES

1

When we see the dancer
move her slim form
in speech purer than speech

we do not see the muscles strain
and reach;

we do not think of years unlearning
earth's hard facts.
or of the sweat it takes
to break the pattern the mind makes
of stone and apple-fall,
or how the will is set and firm
in snipping the tough warp of gravitation

leaving space to conceive her body's acts
of delicate free levitation.

2

Admiring a xivth century arras,
woven perhaps by some less faithful dame,
we see a gentle fable of the time:
virgin and unicorn on silken grass.

The shapely doll-house landscape stands bemused;
the beast, a sublimate of darker gods,
moves ceremoniously. Beyond the woods
the hunter's hounds stand marble-still, confused.

Tracing the symmetry of peacock trees
eyed with such fruit as gardens never grew
we can be charmed and, half-amused, agree
about that other time's naiveties

Yet, in the ancient stitched design not see
the twin duplicity depicted here,
as maid and unicorn approach the hour
which all their patterned lives would make them flee:

How stealthily the girl must loose her fears
of horn, and of its fleshy referent
and all imaginings of brute affront,
that innocence may be as it appears.

And how the timid unicorn, all taut
with nerves that know the smallest shift of leaf
must now renounce all learning of his life,
and wilfully walk forward to be caught.

    3

           When I was Penelope
               I lived
               for the one gold day
               in a winter's rain

        unravelled every night
        what I had learned of pain

I searched for the faces of friends and lovers
        on buses
               in the street crowd
secretly
        I was proud
        I could make one
        fat drop of sun
                burst its warm juices on my head.

So prized and lovely that,
        it could sustain
        my work of slyly tearing, thread by thread
        what I had learned

of enemies
        and the heart's maze
                and the demon-perilled journey between
first   and second thought

        4
So the old boy came home,
burst brawling into the anteroom,
interrupting forever covert yawns
scurrilous anecdotes
        sweet songs —

the place at once a melee of kicked bums,
hacked limbs,
slimy with blood of those who hadn't been quick
or didn't bounce far enough on the first kick —

Blood to the elbows, he howled:
"Woman, where in hell's my towel?"

He believed her finally, and her slaves;
examined the tapestry she wove and unwove;
accepted her as loyal;

but there was distance in his eyes,
veiled inattention she had come to recognize
in suitors, begging her for loving looks
while mentally counting vines and flocks.

He dozed over wine,
made love indifferently;

his eyes kept turning, sucking, to the sea;
he would start, "Did I tell you about the time—"

then shrug, and go out to gossip with his men.

In a matter of weeks
he was off again

and Penelope, left with her flawed work
had it to face:

She could have spun her hanging of her hair
or made her bed a market thoroughfare—
he didn't care.

And it came to a choice:
whether to let her age-long labour fall,
grow old and bitter, turn her face to the wall,
or somehow to gather will,
begin unpicking the pattern of her life,
and weave again
               designs
                       of innocence and disbelief ...

83   FOR SELECTED FRIENDS

Work one face of a stone
only
so I can always have you:
at times I am one-dimensional,
love on paper.

It's easier to photograph you
with my mind
arresting you at mid-point
in some brilliant exposition
before discovery moves you
off the surface.

Although I know you're
a cave splendid with crystals
and white bats,
sometimes I am
afraid to go there.

84 NEITHER DID TREES RINGING

Neither did trees ringing with birds
grow from his open-palmed hands

nor could his head
encompass weather
(drift of clouds under the wide arch
of his cranium
so that parched travellers
might walk through the lanes of his eyes
into kinder country)

nor did his heart grow
a thickness of grapes
in its own winepress
and his mouth flowing with cultured sunlight

Only his hair greyed
and sleep like a slow wrestler
demanded his blessing

which he could not give
Even with children in his arms
his shoulders ached and prickled
for birds

frosting
green things he passed
with his grey hair
he felt blossoms
seeded within him

Neither did his heart
pumping sour wine
ever cease to labour to fill
the cups for a wedding

85 PATIENCE

The game he plays is so exacting
that I've often seen him
strung out like a structural limb
supporting tons and traffic —
and his lumped gargoyle face
crimson with strain.
the muscles sharp as bitten pickles
and his poor eyes popping tears.

From time to time he'll open his door
and demand something preposterous
sent in — snails
cooked in Tibetan wine,
virgins with babies
already inside them.

When the game goes well
he sometimes takes a break,
goes outside with his dirty clothes
wide open and starts the street
dancing like trees.

One has to make allowances.
After all, if he makes it
come out right,
all broken things will become whole
and nothing alive will ever again
be brought low.

86 GROWING THE SEASONS
(FOR DOROTHY LIVESAY)

Brown tough
and delicate
the satin skin
underground
over the pleated green
is always breaking,
is always ready to be
torn open
like gift wrap

*"the large golden Trumpet
Daffodil should be considered,
If a patch of grass
is available
that can be left uncut
Likewise the oft repeated advice
to scatter the bulbs
and plant them where they fall,
while excellent in theory,
makes rather heavy work"*
(I dream
of being stoned to death
and am resurrected
pulling thistles)

The long light of the sun
even the pressure
of starlight
beats my nape and shoulders.
Thirty summers rock me
on my knees
blinded with migraine.
Hazel woman I envy you
your fifty
summers of nasturtiums.

All winter snow falls
in the body's quiet spaces.
I am an hourglass woman
half filled with snow
but she
makes spring in the ivory season
of her bones,
that spare geometry
is feathery with flowers.
O see
her thumbs are hyacinths
her collarbone a necklace
of bright dayseyes.

87 FOR ROBERT BLY SAYING POEMS

There should be
a flat drum at his belly
and wind-chimes spinning from the hem
of his Indian sun-eyed cape
when this late last son
of the medicine show man
makes his pitch for
the one true physic
that could cost us everything
we think we own

Laid in some dreamy Edna
in a cell-small town
conceived in the warm reek of snake oil
chicken fat, sarsaparilla
(What *was* the girl thinking of,
I ask you? :
diversions of the frontier)
and up pops Robert,

a standing broad jump
at the lip of every prairie
and between deserts
he sets his camp
negotiates the weather
casts his first lines
into the crowd

The pitch is away —
that heavy butterfly
(Oh Dr. Conroy, look!)
and apple pie isn't in it
apple pie is an afterthought

to Robert Bly,
the allamerican hot dog is
a footnote to his flying hands

There should be a flat drum
at his belly or hung below
so his thighs could manoeuvre a rhythm
leaving his casting hands free

He is not saying,
What will you do if?
He's telling you what you will do if,
what you will do when

There should be a crackle of thunder
and wind running like a dog
among the listeners

88   REGARD TO NERUDA

When I heard that
the world's greatest poet
was running for president:
being north american
I would have laughed, until
I thought of the campaign trek
over country that was
his blood and bed,
the persistent human song
for which he became
rivers, harps of forests,
metallic skies of cities.
and I thought also
of the tenderness implied
in his handshake.

Could I see with his high vision
(man with thick hands and belly
full of good things)
the naked feet of beginnings,
the sons of rare minerals
transforming the earth,
could I wash my country
with songs that settle
like haloes on the constituents,
I'd campaign
to be prime minister
without kisses.

Often now I forget
how to make love
but I think I am ready
to learn politics.

89   MOONWALK SUMMER

Even before our waking
eyes, their boots walking
stirring that millions of years asleep
soil, seeded
a garden ready to spring
complete in the mind's curve
before waking

Days, the burden of miracle
is heavy,
the mind bends,
but mornings before waking
the moon balloon at the world's lips
is balanced on breath,
is easy as summer
walking

The Ship returning phallic to water
comforts the men
who for generations have dreamed
their outward ships phallic

But the craft
of the actual touch,
frail and ungainly
and sprouting sensitive extensions,
opened like a woman
to bring forth men

Women are accustomed
to hold in our sleep
the whole curve,
birth, silence, again birth

So these sunyellow mornings
before my waking
that fabled desert world blooms
a whole flower
of human working

90 SOLSTICES

In our parish
the sun spoke twice a year:

Once in high summer,
a long colloquy with his chosen
(the priests of summer
never knew their calling
till his voice sent them reeling
white-eyed through the dry streets)
When they passed near us
we could faintly hear
the rasp of the sun's voice
crackling between
their temple walls,

And once at the flyspeck
dead end of the year
with the sky low as a ceiling,
to everyone came the sun,
a voice in a blind funnel,
a tiny thunder
at the blank wall of the ear,
giving instructions
on dying and being born.

91   HAUNTING

Between the Esso station
and the Green Jade restaurant
my grandmother's house still stands,
penetrated by ivy.
Fruit trees grown wild
darken the windows where
Aunt Lily, or was it Isabelle,
once saw a dark lady
vanish in the upstairs hall.

A gap in the crooked
teeth of industry,
the house is sinister
enough now for ghosts,
for Grandma and all the Aunts
to walk without
their crinkled, flower-talcumed flesh
that scented all the upstairs rooms.

92 TOWARD A PRAGMATIC PSYCHOLOGY

Every night at midnight the house falls.
Stairs fold like pleated paper.
The walls slide down
a straight incline
like wooden rain.
Pigeons desert the eaves and fly east.
The roof is swept away
a pointed arc
beaching at last on some intersection
under trolley wires and pruned trees.

Every morning we have to
compose the house anew
paper the walls
reinvent principles of engineering
mouths, places to sit.
Every night we lie down
without prayer.

93   TV

"You'll do better tomorrow"
they tell me
as suppressing my shakes
I step down from meters of air

—and I had thought the test was over
when I'd done it once

"Everywhere she looks
she thinks she's in Death Valley"
I hear them whisper,
less concerned for me
than pleased at insighting the trouble

Only last night
I saw an Asian child, both legs
and a hand torn off,
swing her intractable weight
between two rails.

94 JESUS CHILD

Coming unexpectedly to the edge
of ocean and the known world
she took one extra step,
tottered in midspace.
Sea drank her, sky
sucked her hair.
Afraid any minute she'd dissolve
and fall as rain —
afraid too that she wouldn't,
but be caught, clapped again
in a bone cage,
submissive as her mother's
budgie bird —
she kited, trying for a compass
or a handy wind.

Then a benign head
from a lithograph appeared
to explain everything,
sea, love, sky, terror.
Like a bird she chirped
joyful phrases, water and seed
grew holy in her song.

Now she practices
jumping from cliff tops
and flutters at passers-by
"Come let me take you"
where no one can go
except alone.

95 LETTER TO THE MAJORITY

We are not what you think we are.
In another space
enclosing another space
we have grown
whole crops of quiet.
Even our laughter
laughing at ourselves
has been too soft for you to hear.
You have thought us a mirror
to your torments
and your homely pleasures.
You have been watching
motion on a screen only.

You send us casual
directives—Eat me, Drink me.
We brush your language
from the pages of books.
It is a momentary diversion.
The only way you can
speak to us
is by speaking to the whole world.

FIVE DIPTYCHS

96 THE BURNINGS
    (SAIGON, BOSTON, SAN FRANCISCO, PRAGUE)

Romantics make poetry
of moth and flame

the gilded eyes
of desire

but the bumbling thing
strangling heavy
with spilled kerosene
and a near candle

oh what a flying cork—
screwing sizzling coal!

down like a dropped jewel
from a woman's hair

the moth is tuned
to moonlight.
our cosmetic candle
painted on the night
confounds him,
spins him lost

It is a wrecker's light
that downs him.

no
animal
conceive the perfect motive
to be
        SInaI
                ArArAt
the whole wheeling
h o r i z o n
implicit in gesture

but when his hair
curly as black Adams
hissed and sparkled
he screamed

for someone anyone
to take his God hood
and his crucifixion
clothes of fire

cries
       blow breath
to the fire-beating
bush of nerves

too late
to put on again
the habit of flesh

the standing fire
goes ahead
the beacon pointing
out of bondage

169

97 TO CAPTURE PROTEUS

River of milk and stars
I float in
tidal river

weeds curl around my fingers
long shapes of fish
swim also beside me

fish graze
the soles of my feet

In water
all shapes are separate
as my limbs are apart from me
moving like other swimmers

A splash, and I'm Hydra
in a galaxy of foam

swirled in the cold prick
of bubbles on my underbelly

Whatever is spare strange original
Water makes me
I am a simple tube

a man I love
in every man
why do you shift your eyes
and the known surfaces
of your body?

Whether I love
you, or deny all love
we are separate
only as fingers

Flicker, fish
Bird, start upbeating
And the cherry tree seethes
with a susurrus of wind
among his leaves

How can I hold fast
to that rough body?

Run like water and wind
curl me with fire
I'll hold still
to the man of you

Darling I only want
a long soul-kiss
to my forehead
or maybe to kiss the temples
above your eyes

Dancing the complex of the tides
I am moved
past an estuary
I perceive as an out-
flung extremity of my body
The peopled city
sounds a neural rock
Patterns are made with blocks
of lighted windows
Telephones are dialled
and answered

Proteus I am in love
with the marvellous
cancer you sow
For love I'll bind you
with guitar strings
with staves of music
I'll manacle you
with my woman's thighs
Come, we'll amuse ourselves
with the universal consolation

As water takes me
where landhold falls away
I am aware of caves
where salamanders
that the sun would blacken
sleep in perpetual youth

a man I love
in every man
in love-child's opaque eyes
behind thousands of eyes

My hair floats in the water
separate as water ferns
brushes the mouths
of the sleepers' caves
I float from the river's mouth
on my back
on my back facing
the moon my own mirror

I shall surprise you asleep
and hold you
through all your changes
till you make me
pregnant with the world

98   THE FALCONER

                        Only awake as the sun
                        creates first shapes
                        I go through still-wet grass
                        with the falcon's heavy claws
                        bracketing my wrist
                        but he is hooded still,
                        within the binding-cloth
                        he breathes a world
                        small as a fist,
                        without moving his eyes
                        back and forth needle and pinch
                        pleats in tiny space.

Persistent soft kettle-drum roll
of wind at loose windows —
just enough to keep a baby
from sleeping soundly —
oh keep the blinds down yet,
there's too much light.

                        Before us clouds shiver
                        sprigs of leaves move
                        a small lake is oval like a mirror
                        mirrors the day
                        and the day mirrors water,
                        the day takes the colour of water.

Yawn in the mirror's marine reflection,
an underwater room
drowned in a tidal pool
only a few feet deep.
Writhe with elegant aquatic motions,
not to be reeled up
from the depths of bed.

                The day advances, spreads,
                like water rising
                We move forward
                as though surrounded by our retinue
                We walk as though centring
                a ceremonial of friends
                Ahead at the two corners, starlings,
                behind us a few blown leaves.

                The falcon tastes sky through his hood
                His talon tugs at my wrist
                as though he'd be away
                away and lift me with him.

How to accept the day
the dry hours
the work the whining children
the traffic?   Turn
on the oldest comfort,
the bath of flesh.

                Now at a valley's lip I loose him
                where he glitters up
                He is my high golden eye
                Fields gyre and slide
                copses of trees spin
                the sun flashes on-off
                behind the shutter of his beating wing.

Will we grow old
rocking the creaking furniture of sex?
Perhaps some year
two aged brittle sticks rubbing together
we will ignite again
and burn each other out.
The firemen will say,
"They must have smoked in bed."

                    Now my falcon finds patterns,
paths made by our prey,
green is broken
yellow is broken
brown is broken
their trails impose a wild geometry
like a mandala
He slews, his eye spins
and I quicken moving doubly,
my feet blind on broken ground
my eyes high up
researching leaf and cloud shade.

And find their shelter
where they lie all crossed and curled
into a tense rosette
shutting their eyes and hoping
themselves safe
The falcon, teased
by dragonflies and wild small birds
disdains them
arrows all his blazing
on that earthy prey.

The baby stirs
threshes like a swimmer in its rustling crib
gulps breath
for the day's first cry.

                    But look — they are coupling,
on my strewn ground their shelter
their bodies twine together
like a wheel
So near their end

			they make beginning
			I shall not take them
			Let them be fruitful
			and thus yield us game
			for other seasons.

The baby's cry hooks us at last
draws us up
out of the bed
out of the warm melting
We reach for clothes.

			I call my falcon down
			He angers,
			slashes the sky, wheels, spins
			to make me dizzy
			but I have drawn myself back
			to the grass and the slow ground breezes
			scented with water,
			I shall walk home,
			in the brightness of day
			the hunter will fold his wings
			and accept the hood,
			we shall be pleasantly tired
			and sleep.

99   THE ELECTRIC BOY

Wrapt in his crazy cloth
of junkyard electrodes
clothesline wire
knit copper hair
from shredded extension cords
he is a hedge
a prick of silence
in a bare corner

Students will form lines
at the sound of the first bell
and at the second bell
march
        Late slips
        must be filed in triplicate
Identity numbers will be issued
on admittance

There is danger in becoming
dazzled by the idea
of choreographing anarchy

His life he believes
selfmade
contained in that painstaken
catch-shift armour
This wire breathes me
This wire moves
my heart

Wait for the signal to flash WALK.
Do not run but walk rapidly.
        When the whistle blows
        everyone rise
        and file out singly.

At night he plugs in
to an imaginary battery

The choice of evening TV programs
will be decided by majority vote

At first he would not eat
until they convinced him
the soup was especially ion-rich
a protonplasmic broth
to nourish electrolife

Feedings are every 4 hours.
All formula is prepared
under sterile conditions.

This wire lets me see
and this connection
is my feeling

The executive washroom
may be used only
by those so authorized

but no connection
penetrates within those coils
no touch encounters
flesh

: WHITE : : COLORED :

To break that armature
it will be necessary
to persuade him of
the special beauty of chance
the splendid fragility
of animal life

Order has value in proportion
to the guilty delight
produced by a moment's disorder

Pacification techniques however
often result in
80% casualties
among the civilian population

It is persistently rumoured
that there are ways of "fixing"
computer-based personality tests

For no care can efface
the Janus-pain of love
not even to uncurl
a boy's hand
closed in a wire glove

And those peasants
still still
live
in the teeth
of the war machine

100 JOURNEY OF THE MAGI

They'll not come again,
the instant people,
one born every minute,
pavement everywhere
incredibly swarming

automatic stop and go signals
for traffic.
their machines,
full of passengers,
aroar like a great millrace

their houses intricate
with machinery
for cleaning, heating;
their miles of elaborate plumbing

their families multiplying
uninterrupted generations,
three, four, five children
playing,
and pet dogs and cats

How silently we walk
without echoes
through dust lapping
silk to our ankles

on high ground
thin new grass
pricks up its ears
to the odd fall
of our footsteps

Last night when we made camp
a rat—
we stoned it
being careful to chase it away,
not to kill it
for fear of its parasites

Our camp fire
calls forth the dingoes,
race memories war in them,
fear and desire,
they slaver but keep back—
God knows
which plague they carry

Whole hospitals
full of birthing women,
life crying ringing
through hills of clean rooms —
and even in hived hovels,
unwelcomed,
without gifts

They'll not come again
with their laughing and fighting,
magnificent waste,
growing gardens for pleasure.
studying abstractions

their hands all-gifted
and making and breaking,

they'll never
       come again

The day we had news
of the birth,
the first in two years,
a butterfly was sighted.
Our eyes stung
with colour,
whole species recreated themselves
in minds' shaping.
We set forth

And holy birth
like clean water shining
leads us over the desert
and sick places

to kneel at last
heavy with our small gifts:
the clean seed corn,
the ointment
against certain ills,
the poison and the prayer
against its need

101 MR. HAPPYMAN IS COMING

Mr. Happyman is coming.
Release the streets.
Let them be tongues of green country
or shimmer of heat dance.

On the edge of town now he's
sticking his finger into foxgloves
and licking off pollen.

Down on the beach
he whispers into the earholes of limpets
murmurs into the sea's innumerable ears
until the sea stands up singing,
clapping its white hands.

He is making a gorgeous
ruin of the sun
scattering it to pieces,
one for everyone.

You can hear him in the graveyard
crow like the first daffodil-rooster:
"Oh holy here I flesh you,
I re-enact you,
and have appetite enough
to forage for all the open mouths in earth."

Mr. Happyman is coming.
Bring all the new born children.
In his round mouth he rolls
the names of people without names.

A grand thunder of names
sings through the honeycomb cave of his skull.
Gladly will he be Adam
for all the generations
and give each child a name to grow on.

Bring him your hair and fingernails.
He collects fingernail clippings
of carpenters and ships' joiners,
rolls like a lovesick dog
in the cut hair of women and girls.

He fishes with fishermen
in their grey salt afternoons
then lies down with whales and dolphins
enfolded eye to eye.

Tonight he will sleep
with all the lonely women
arching them into shapes of pride.
The whole world will be rumpled
like bedclothes under him.

Tomorrow he'll be gone to the quiet
where his mind like jewellers' fingers
worships among minutiae
and steeped in black acid
a posture a grimace of pain
he crouches while this world he eats
eats him.

1977

A Stone
Diary

I

102 A STONE DIARY

At the beginning I noticed
the huge stones on my path
I knew instinctively
why they were there
breathing as naturally
as animals
I moved them to ritual patterns
I abraded my hands
and made blood prints

Last week I became
aware of details
cubes of fool's gold
green and blue copper
crystal formations
fossils   shell casts
iron roses   candied gems

I thought of
the Empress Josephine,
the Burning of Troy
between her breasts,
of Ivan the Terrible lecturing
on the virtues of rubies.
They were dilettantes.

By the turn of the week
I was madly in love
with stone. Do you know
how beautiful it is
to embrace stone
to curve all your body
against its surfaces?

Yesterday I began
seeing you as
desirable as a stone
I imagined you coming
onto the path with me
even your mouth
a carved stone

Today for the first time
I noticed how coarse
my skin has grown
but the stones shine
with their own light,
they grow smoother
and smoother

103 RUMOURS OF WAR

In my very early years
I must have heard
ominous news broadcasts
on the radio;
they must have mentioned
the Black Forest

for I dreamed a black forest
moving across a map,
I and my rag doll
caught on the coast edge
of the country
I was too young
even to name

Austria Poland Hungary
would have meant nothing
to me
but the Black Forest
came right up our ravine
down over the mountains

and Raggedy Ann
and I woke screaming
out of the clutch of
evil trees

104 EARLY WINTERS

Under the burned-off mountain
winds died   the forest rangers
packed their sleeping bags
and left for town
trees cracked their knuckles
windows began telling stories

And the child dreamed meteors
spiralling like snowflakes
into the trees

Herbs in the garden died
bees slept in their cells
a late bear tumbled the garbage cans
the creek broke ice
and rushed endlessly past the house

And the child dreamed blue water
green water
and the death of water

Deer on the winter road
wore jewels in their antlers
the spines of the burnt mountain
sifted the snow
like a giant comb

And the child dreamed passionate singers
gathering mountains before them
irresistible as the wind

The sky stayed white all night
the valley rocked
with the speed of the creek
breathing a sound like a shell

And the child dreamed all
trees   mountains
the unknown singers
luminous and falling
as softly as the snow

105 PRIVATE OWNERSHIP

The peacocks scream
on Curlew Island
owned by a Texas Millionaire
guarded by Fierce Dogs
and Peacocks
(don't beach a boat there
you'll be savaged by mastiffs,
lashed by the clacking
tails of peacocks)
Peacocks are more alert
than dogs, but stupid:
gulls set them off
or mocking crows
or boys across the channel
on the public beach.
Soon there's a wild concert
Gulls Crows Boys and Peacocks
screaming again and again
till the Dogs catch
the hysteria, bark insanely.
Out comes the Millionaire,
paunch wobbling or
bony fist shuddering
(of course I've never seen him,
he's probably a Thing of Beauty
his physique as carefully guarded
as Curlew Island)
Nobody's ever seen him
but we hear his voice:
Shuddup, you gawdam dogs !
Shuddup !

106 INHERITANCE

Annie McCain bequeathed to me
her lace:
tatting crocheting
yards and yards of
ecru and cream and white
spiderweb pattern pineapple
doilies and tablecloth edging

She must have imagined me
in the citrus smell
of furniture polish
gleaming walnut and oak
pouring tea from a silver pot

She should have known even then
I'd be something else
useless at owning things
up to my head in books

But she gave me lace.
I'd rather have had
her old corsets
that I fastened for her
with mighty heaves,
or her brass bed
where I slept in the warm
dent she made
early mornings
I'd rather have her rockingchair
I coveted half my life

Twenty-five years in tissue
wraps, Annie McCain's lace
runs through my all-thumbs
like something I can't
even regret.
It's turning slowly amber
like her beautiful hair
that never went grey
in a long life of making

107   NIGHTMARE

Edgar Allan Poe &
Disney combined
couldn't have done it
better: the tall black house
the dungeon
the secret book

Later, the pale determined
men with dogs.
I try to cry out:
I'm harmless!
but the words can't
get through my fangs.

108 CHACABUCO, THE PIT

(Information filtered out of Chile: political
prisoners formerly held in the stadium at Santiago
have been transported to a Nazi-type concentration
camp set up in a disused nitrates mine somewhere
on the Atacama desert.)

               EVERYTHING SHOULD BE DONE
QUIETLY AND EFFECTIVELY TO INSURE
THAT ALLENDE DOES NOT LAST THE NEXT
CRUCIAL SIX MONTHS.
—from 18-point plan submitted by International
Telegraph and Telephone Co. to the White House, USA.

               CONTACT TRUSTWORTHY SOURCES
WITHIN THE CHILEAN ARMED FORCES.
—from point 7, above.

          I shall speak to the Lord of Heaven
where he sits asleep.
—from an ancient Mayan prayer.

Atacama desert:
by day the sun lets down
his weight   everyone wears
a halo   everything quivers
sharp-sided dust refracts
blurred glitter between
creased squinting eyelids;
by night the land is naked
to the farthest reaches
between galaxies
that vacuum sucks
heat: the land is
cold to the utter bone.

Carefully now (place
records on a turntable)
remember those 1940s movies
where virgins were sacrifices
to volcanoes: here is
that same
    ceremonial
        suspenseful
            approach:
we are approaching
        Chacabuco
            the pit.

Notice first the magnificent sunset,
the stars, the clouds of Magellan.
Note that here as in all human places
prayer has been uttered.

Watch until morning
burns the sky white.
Wooden shacks persevere
in the dry air,
their corners banked with dust;
a grid of streets prints
an ominous white shadow
on your eyelids;
it leads
to the pit.

A huge, gouged cavity
flickering like a bad film,
the whole scene twitching
on and off
in and out of existence:
is God blinking? are you
shuttering your eyes, tourista?

I shall speak to the lord of heaven
where he sits asleep

there are men in that pit
imagine that they are chained
(they may be)
starving (they are)
watched over by jailers
with faces blank
as a leached brain

Working, that sallow bitter rock
ground to glass
powder enters their lungs
nostrils eyes pores
Sleeping, they dream of eating
rock, sucking juice from it
pissing nitrate dust

Moments of darkness film
their eyes, they stumble
in negative light
and the blows of whips

* * *

Do they remember
who they are? patriots
       believers
             . builders

collective dreamers who woke
to find all their good wishes
happening faster
than they could move,
the people outreaching the planners
factory workers running

the factories
children wearing moustaches
of milk

Forgetting to keep guns beside their pillows
forgetting to bribe generals
breathing long breaths of peace
organizing anti-Fascist song festivals
instead of militia
seeing the people stand at last
upright in mellow light like a sound harvest
they forgot lifetimes of exile
years of held breath and stealth
seeing so many strong
they forgot the strength of I.T.&T.
United Fruit Co.
    Anaconda
who do not easily give up
what they have taken.

* * *

Some one decides
who shall eat
who shall not eat
who shall be beaten
and on which
parts of his body

Some one decides
who shall be starved
who shall be fed
enough to sustain
another day's torture

A man decides.
That man does not breathe dust:
he is dust.

* * *

Choirs of young boys
exquisitely trained
sing hymns in cathedrals;
jellyfish swim in the ocean
like bubbles of
purity made tangible;
whole cities lie open
to the stars;
women bake bread;
fruit trees unfold their blossoms
petal by petal;
we are continually born

but these, captive, stumble
in gross heat
in stupor of pain:
they are the fingers sliced off
when the wood was cut,
the abortions born living;
they are the mangled
parts of our bodies
screaming to be
reunited.

* * *

'If I forget thee, O Zion'

Let statesmen's tongues lock
between their jaws,

let businessmen's cheque hands
be paralyzed,
let musicians stop building
towers of sound,
let commerce fall
in convulsions:
we have deserved this.

* * *

Staircases ascending
through caverns
clefts in the root sockets
of mountains, opening
onto ocean's foot:
we have all been there,
that journey, its
hardships its surprises
stay in our cells
our footprints in clay
splayed: we were burdened.

Remember breathing on fire
a cautious husbandry
then suddenly sparks
bursting upward
like dolphins leaping
in the sunlight path
of the first boat
we had song
        mathematics
              magic

Even for torturers we have done this
journey, broken
ourselves like crumbs,

pumped children into wombs,
heaved them out,
laid stone on stone;
we forgive each other
our absurdities,
casually accept splendour;
we forgive even death

but these places
of death slowly inflicted
we can't forgive, but writhe
coiling in on ourselves
to try to forget, to deny:
*we have travelled so far
and these are still with us?*

Even now in our cities
churches   universities
pleasant lawns   we are
scrabbling with broken nails
against rock, we are
dying of flies and disease.
Until that pus is drained
we are not healed.

* * *

'And the dead shall be raised incorruptible'

When their names are called
will you answer,
will I?

for bread on the table
for salt in the bread
for bees in the cups

of flowers
will you answer to their names?

For I tell you the earth
itself is a mystery
which we penetrate constantly
and our people a holy mystery
beyond refusal

And the horrors of the mind
are the horrors of
what we allow to be done
and the grace of the soul
is what we determine shall be
made truly among us.   Amen.

109 LEONARD GEORGE AND, LATER, A ROCK BAND

I

Do you know you can
talk to trees
do you know
stones are alive
do you know birds
fish   water   a song
for every position of the sun

In lieu of guns or tears
he raises these
against the bricked eyes
of the speculators

His memory rooted
in specific magic
of land alive
When the trees go
he won't be here

To speak from the cramped edges
against their assumption
of his death
he says first his true name
and the names of his father
and grandfather

With those syllables
unique   unshared
he brings it altogether
against them
a man whole
in the broken world

2

Netting the random air
with their drums,
cymbals, demanding electrons,
for them sooner
than for us it comes together,
a geodesic web of sound
in which their freedom's
their contained dimension.

Now with their easy will,
with the power
of having it whole,
they move it outward
to contain us.
We are altogether
touching in the warm electric
balloon, dependent
on a cord, a plug.

110 NOTES FROM FURRY CREEK

1

The water reflecting cedars
all the way up
deep sonorous green—
nothing prepares you
for the ruler-straight
log fallen across
and the perfect
water fall it makes
and the pool behind it
novocaine-cold
and the huckleberries
hanging
like fat red lanterns

2

The dam, built
by coolies, has outlived
its time; its wall
stained sallow
as ancient skin
dries in the sun

The spillway still
splashes bright spray
on the lion
shapes of rock
far down below

The dam foot
is a pit
for the royal animals
quiet and dangerous
in the stare
of sun and water

3

When the stones swallowed me
I could not surface
but squatted
in foaming water
all one curve
motionless,
glowing like agate.

I understood the secret
of a monkey-puzzle tree
by knowing its opposite:

the smooth and the smooth
and the smooth takes,
seduces your eyes
to smaller and smaller
ellipses;
reaching the centre
you become
stone, the perpetual
lavèd god.

III THE EARTH SINGS MI-FA-MI

'... so we can gather even from this
that MIsery and FAmine reign on
our habitat.'
JOHANNES KEPLER, a footnote to *Harmonice Mundi.*

Outside the U.S. consulate
in freezing wind
the street theatre group
arranges space within
the crowd

The girl who represents
the Vietnamese people
wears a black body
stocking and a mask
I thought at first
patronizing
but as the mime unfolds
its over-human contours
and its broken eyes
immovable
become a perfect image
for us all

Those of us near
the players sing with them
softly shouldering aside
our inhibitions
Ho Ho Ho Chi Minh
hoping our soft noise
will spread outward
from the centre

But the wind screams
and the earth spinning
like notes uttered
like whipped wires
the earth sings Mi-Fa-Mi

January 1973

112 FACE

it's said a leader loses
something seen
in the flesh smaller
than his image on
the cool grey t.v.
choosing words
precisely as specified
pincers and screws;
seeing in the street's
light, his egg face
greased with anxiety,
tension of a present crowd
hostile, is more whole-
some: seeing a leader
sweat in the face
of the people.

113 COAST RANGE

Just north of town
the mountains start to talk
back-of-the-head buzz
of high stubbled meadows
minute flowers
moss gravel and clouds

They're not snobs, these mountains,
they don't speak Rosicrucian,
they sputter with
billygoat-bearded creeks
bumsliding down
to splat into the sea

they talk with the casual
tongues of water
rising in trees

They're so humble they'll let you
blast highways through them
baring their iron and granite
sunset-coloured bones
broken for miles

And nights when
clouds foam on a beach
of clear night sky,
those high slopes creak
in companionable sleep

* * *

Move through grey green
aurora of rain

to the bare fact:
The land is bare.

Even the curly opaque Pacific
forest, chilling you full awake
with wet branch-slaps,
is somehow bare
stainless as sunlight:

The land is what's left
after the failure
of every kind of metaphor.

* * *

The plainness of first things
trees
gravel
rocks
naive root atom
of philosophy's first molecule

The mountains reject nothing
but can crack
open your mind
just by being intractably there

Atom: that which can not
be reduced

You can gut them
blast them
to slag
the shapes they've made in the sky
cannot be reduced

114 DARK

I tell you the darkness comes down
like arrows and hunger
I tie knots in my hair
to remember other empires
The world falls through my forehead
resistlessly as rain

I must tell you I can not
always move with decorum
The darkness comes down like meteors
petals of hot black
I escape burning only because
I am the darkness

II

115 SONG

If I take you to my island
you'll have to remember
to speak quietly
you'll have to remember
sound carries over water
You must come by night
we'll walk through the dark
orchards to the sea
and gather crystal jellyfish
from the black water
we'll lie on the sand
and feel the galaxy
on our cheeks and foreheads
you'll have to remember
to wear warm clothing
follow where I go
and speak very softly
if I take you

116 ANEMONES

Under the wharf at Saturna
the sea anemones
open their velvet bodies

chalk black
      and apricot
           and lemon-white

they grow as huge
and glimmering
      as flesh chandeliers

under the warped
and salt-stained wharf
   letting down
      their translucent mouths
                of arms

even the black ones
have an aura
like an afterimage of light

Under our feet
   the gorgeous animals
      are feeding
           in the sky

117 OCTOPUS

The octopus is beautifully
functional as an umbrella;
at rest a bag of rucked skin
sags like an empty scrotum
his jelled eyes sad and bored

but taking flight: look
how lovely purposeful
in every part:
the jet vent smooth
as modern plumbing
the webbed pinwheel of tentacles
moving in perfect accord
like a machine dreamed
by Leonardo

118 CRANEFLIES IN THEIR SEASON

Struggling in the grass
or splayed against walls and fences,
they seem always somehow askew.
Even their flights in air
appear precarious
and all their moves seem
to be accidents.

Dead, they form windrows
of bent wires,
broken delicate parts
of some unexplained machine.
And the wind sweeps them
like evidence of an accident
out of sight.

119 HERMIT CRABS

In a pool maybe the size
of a man's forearm
there are hundreds of them,
like curled amber
snail shells scuttling sideways
like no snails.
You can just see
their brindle legs
fine as the teeth of a fine-tooth
tortoiseshell comb.
Five of them might
cover my fingernail,
but poke one
and he'll put out pincers
thin as bronze wire
and dare you
to do it again.

120 SLUGS

        Yellow grey
                boneless things
     like live phlegm
heaving themselves
gracelessly
across sidewalks
laboured
as though the earth
were not their element
oozing their viscid mess
    for godsake don't
               step
                      there
ugh ugh
horrible pulp

:two of them:
the slime from their bodies
makes a crystal rope
       suspending
them   in air
     under
   the apple tree

   they are twined
      together
in a perfect spiral
   flowing
             around
   each other
       spinning
  gently
      with their motions
Imagine
   making love like that

121 SUSPENDED

When you choose silence
I shall be like
the last rain
        drop
on a tree branch
  waiting to fall

Imagine that I contain
     branch   tree
  butterflies   snakes
the entire forest
    a sun
hardly a pin-prick's size
    but bright enough
    to spear your eye

122 WRESTLING

Lover I must
approach you as Jacob
to his angel,
rough with that need.
Yes I will
pin you down,
force answers from you;
I will make sense
of you, place you
like a planet
or constellation
in my known zodiac:
First fall.

123 BIRTHDAYS

1

You say you were born
a time and place
foreign to me;
i can't imagine
where you come from
though you wear your past
like articulated flesh,
a body learned
and exercised

how have you disguised
your battles
that i see
you without scars,
assume them only
as one assumes
the tough mechanics
of heart and bowels

i know there
must have been darkness
fish thrashing in blood
that stinging slash
where light breaks
: metamorphoses

2

just as you breaking
into, displace me,
thrust me under
my own past, i have
to go through

it all again;
nothing will come out
any differently,
but i will

: one of those
places where the surface
breaks like water
clashes and chops
of light, far under
everything is shifted
everything moves

   3

all nerves ending
in air make the shape
of a birthday, the shape
set out: 'Go'
some other stranger says

and walking flying
you move toward
more birthdays
than anyone
expects or celebrates

124 GREETINGS FROM THE INCREDIBLE SHRINKING WOMAN

it's not that
i'm getting smaller
(i thought so at first)
but that the continent's
expanding, stretching
like silly putty
or like a movie
seen in a dream

landmarks, even back fences,
recede; where i am
is always empty

i used to see myself
at the land's edge
waiting maybe to be
flicked off,
to thrash like a fish
in the saltchuck

now it's miles from
my house even
to the Fraser River
which is immense,
swollen like throat-veins

and the landscape continues
to pull out
while i do nothing

just by standing
here, i'm dwindling
to a dot.
(actually it's that
i'm finally learning
perspective)

125 ANNIVERSARY LETTER TO PABLO

That first time
on the moongravel
they jumped like clumsy fawns.
They were drunk in love
with their own history;
Satori flash lighted
their indelible footprints.

But you warmed the moon
in a loving cup,
in the thawing
water of your eyes,
you the man who moves
under the hill,
the man who kisses stone.

Custodian of footsteps
and magnets,
you take mineral glitter
in the cup
of your hand,
it becomes veins.
You own also the moon
now where they touched.

126 LETTER TO PABLO 2

Even on this spatter
of islands
would you find finger bones
washed up on beaches,
heelprints round as embraces
in the salt rock?

You would know where
the clamshell middens are;
you would be plunged
so wholly in that feast
the cooking fire would burn
still in the deep bowl
of your belly.

Even here between the edges
of the elements
you would be crouched
transmuting delicate fossils
out of foam.

127 LETTER TO PABLO 3

Honouring your dead
with fat of meat
with well-crusted bread
with honey and garlic,
old man licking oil
off your thumbs and belching,
you are more lustrous
than flowers.
Carnations, poppies,
their spice and bravura
fall in a dusting
of petals shaken;
you move past the image
to honour the belly
the hands   the jaws and teeth,
the incense of cooking
the sacrament of bread.

128 LETTER TO PABLO 4

It isn't easy
to keep moving thru
the perpetual motion
of surfaces,
the web of skin and glances

Are you there
always at the centre
like Buddha contemplating
the heart
of the plural self?
:   constant joy
like a fountain
still even in motion

All my life I wanted
that holy water
to well like stigmata
in my palms.
the skin the skin
is so subtle
and so hard to evade

129 LAST LETTER TO PABLO

Under the hills and veins water
comes out like stars;
your spirit
fleshy palpable
mines in the earth
dung and debris of generations;
curled shells
rags of leaves
impress your palms

I imagine you
a plateau city
spangled with frost,
a blue electric wind
before nightfall
that touches and takes
the breath away

How many making love
in the narrow darkness
between labours
how many bodies laid
stone upon stone
generations of fire and dirt
before you broke from us
a whole branch flowering

Cancer the newscast said,
and coma, but
what of the sea
also full of bones
and miracles
they said was your
last prison?

What of your starward-riding
cities creaking again
with steel?   How long
is death?

We are weary of atrocities;
the manure of blood
you said grows
something so frightful
only you could look:
you smoothing wounds
we shudder from—
bloody leather
face forming in mud

Always earth was
your substance:
grain, ores and bones
elements folded in power
humans patient as time
and weather;
now you too lie with skeletons
heaped about you;
our small crooked hands
touch you for comfort

From the deep hollows
water comes out like stars;
you are changing, Pablo,
becoming an element
a closed throat of quartz
a calyx
imperishable in earth

As our species bears
the minute electric
sting, possibility,
our planet carries Neruda
bloodstone
dark jewel of history
the planet carries you
a seed patient as time.

III

130 I.D.

    i want to say
    tell me
    who you are,
    and you give me
    a clear answer,
    who you are

    then i think of
    the question reversed
    like a knife
    bladed toward me
    tell me
    who you are

    : i'm a blunder
    a mouth, crying
    a figure running
    with hands upright
    at right angles
    to the arms

    and i think after
    all i won't
    ask you
    who you are

131 SPITBALL

His hands flicker
brown on the white
costume, the green arena;
a shuttling dance,
all stations touched
Earth, thighs,
heart, the head
covering, the mouth
also moves, chewing
herbs and invocations.
The hands weave wind,
the watchers' tension,
prayers, sweat
from the forehead,
and unseen in the swift
dazzle of motion
the magic spittle
points the ball.

132 LEVITATION

It's only belief
sets us up in contradiction
to the universe;
even just standing still
we're going
against the grain

Last night the student
talking about writing:
his body began to curve
to cave over me
I raised my hands
for his weight
I thought maybe we could
crumple together
painlessly

——suddenly straightened
and fell full length
away from me
striking the back of his head
like wood breaking and I standing there
had not saved
that blow

People who knew how
counted pulse beats,
massaged, but not until
he came back to his eyes
could he lift off
the flat surface

It's only thinking we can
lets us defy the law
of gravity;
even standing
talking about writing
is a kind of
Indian rope trick

133   100

    Yes he is full now
    like an articulated shell,
    fragile, enclosing liquid.
    The slightest thing
    brims his eyes:
    any emotion
    or a minute lapse
    of memory, self-doubt;
    his lips tremble
    like black moths' wings,
    his eyes blue
    as watered milk startle
    through lenses of tears.
    He cannot speak
    to you, to anyone,
    without these tears
    surprising him.
    His hand inky with veins
    falters toward your wrist,
    your arm: touch
    anchors him here, upright.
    There is an urgent message
    fluttering
    like his pulse,
    a prayer, a summation.
    Always, from breath to breath,
    he is saying goodbye.

134 TO A WOMAN WHO DIED OF 34 STAB WOUNDS

I can see it as though I'd been there,
you pouring beer and talking,
your heavy scarlet smile
held out like a credit card.
Glances would cross behind your back
(you'd have been quite spectacular
then, in the way a reconstruction
of the San Francisco Opera House
would be spectacular)
They wouldn't know
that milky velvet you affected
was your true face.

In your prime you'd seduce anyone,
woman or man, considering that
the friendly thing to do.
Your murderer couldn't believe
so much pride could survive
in flesh gone soft.
At the end, coiling, striking,
his rage was for himself,
for his fine body failing
to humble your sagging sixty.

135 REFLECTING SUNGLASSES

Circles of sky
and storefronts in my face—
look through me:
lattice of moving air
chrome   sunburst   faces—
I'm a see-through woman
proof enough of
the proposition that we're all
mostly
empty space.
I swing along carrying
tunnels of vision
through the imaginary fabric
of my brain.
Lean closer and you'll see
you looking out
from me.

136 CITY SLIDE / 1

The fish pushes the
fine net into
one of the large
holes of the coarse net

We arrange spaces
within
spaces
sixes and sevens
sticks and stones
inside us
the large holes
and the fine holes
are silted
with data

Arranging my rectangular
soapbox
between a mens
and a stone lion
thereby eclipsing the sun
for anything shorter than me,
I declaim:
My Fellow Conspirators

Citizens, file your teeth
the big ones
and the small ones.
he's only a string man
destroy him
with terrible smiles

137 CITY SLIDE / 2

For Hugh Jordan

You are strolling thru downtown
with spicy pinks
braided into your moustache.
Your girl being surfeited with answers,
her expression becomes almost severe.
Your little son is bare naked.

Having broken down all the official buildings
by standing against them doing isometrics,
you are unconcerned that the sky
could want to eat you.
You might even toss a few peanuts
into its lewdly stretching jaws.

138 CITY SLIDE / 3

Wilfred Barrett regards the street
as his apartment
and statues
as very tall acquaintances.
From a gum wrapper's viewpoint
the world's an intimate:
he can't understand
about jaywalking.

Wilfred Barrett's the lost
dollar bill
of a bad conscience.
He is the face that remains
beautiful
when everything else has gone bad,
that keeps rising out
of your crotch and bosom,
warm places where it clings
like an unwanted pet.
Wilfred Barrett tempts me
to sentimentality,
tempts me to imagine myself
giving smiles
as if they were jewels and bread.

Wilfred Barrett's a great
respecter of symbols,
reacting to uniforms
as a dog to fleas.
Confident of pavement,
he accepts a cigarette
or a Vag B bust
with equal poise.

Philosophy breaks in him
like bubbles
struggling up through mash.
Head up against
the sooty sun,
he turns your patronage
into a wound, a memory
of guilty love.

139   CITY SLIDE / 4

One day we decided
to recycle the courthouse fountain.
Dozens of people pitched in.
We dismantled the Disney lights
and the computer,
chipped out the bland-coloured tiles
but they lost all their lustre
as soon as they dried.
The sculptures were a dead loss,
bastards of neither
art nor nature.
We broke them down for mosaics
and donated everything
to kindergartens.
But no one could find
the big magnolia tree
that used to stand there.

140 CITY SLIDE / 5

A vine at my window
scratches only gently

the city breathes like
a warm herbivorous mammal

violence among the cells
only a vague pain
below consciousness

the animal sleeps
waiting unknowingly

for a virus
from another climate
to test its viability

141 CITY SLIDE / 6

Love is an intersection
where I have chosen
unwittingly to die

Next year the blue lights
will still be here
lighting up columns of rain

I'll be in a room
in this same city
with my sick headache
reflecting on accidents
of all kinds

142 CITY SLIDE / 7

There is another level
I almost remember:
streets unfold
like the gestures of fountains
graceful as water's
necessities
down where the lighted towers
spiral to vegetable
roots unthreatening
there are cliffs in the city
you will not fall.
but climbing
you will suddenly again
put down your foot *here*.
As you said
(and how could you know
already the grey
hardening in your limbs)
——Christ O Christ, no one lives long.

143 IT HAPPENS EVERY DAY

children crawl into
dumped refrigerators;
trappers alone on snowfields
step in their own snares;
women court dangerous men
who will beat them to death.

on the other hand
it isn't the landlord
who dies when a tenement burns;
the housewife who puts up
botulism in jars
takes her whole family with her;
hunters who wear red jackets
still get shot.

144 KITCHEN MURDER

Everything here's a weapon:
i pick up a meat fork,
imagine
plunging it in,
a heavy male
thrust

in two hands
i heft a stone-
ware plate, heavy
enough?

rummage the cupboards:
red pepper, rape-
seed oil, Drano

i'll wire myself
into a circuit:
the automatic perc,
the dishwater, the
socket above the sink

i'll smile an electric
eel smile:
whoever touches
me is dead.

145 INTERSECTION

At Fraser & Marine, slapped
by the wind from
passing traffic

light standards, trolleys
everything has edges
too real to touch

taxis unload at the hotel
the Gulf station fills them up

the Lego apartment block
is sharp as salt

And the sunset is tea rose
colour strained, clarified
between navy-blue clouds,
the moon in its first
immaculate crescent

it's an axis
   double intersection
      transparencies

the thumb end
where you press
and the whole universe twirls out
a long seamless skin
a rill of piano music

  * * *

the calla lily is seamless
yet divided

that cream skin wall
deceives the eye
following round and around
like fingers on ivory

refractions hook under
the eyelashes
you imagine that you can see
honeycombs
                jewels
                      individual cells

texture reveals nothing;

to touch is to bruise

* * *

diesel trucks negotiate
left turns,
their long trailers creaking

headlights spurt
at the green signals

it was just here
at this bus stop
I lost my glove
my forty-cent transfer
my book
of unwritten profundities

I tell you they fell upward !
I saw them
        glinting
                catching light
from the thin, solid moon

* * *

The Blue Boy Motor Hotel
advertises:
try our comfortably
refurbished rooms
with color TV

the clouds are ink-blue
in the west

mercury lights lie along
the streets' contours
like strings of blue rhinestones

the bus stop bench
is painted blue, it
advertises Sunbeam bread

Don't touch the bench
it could burn you
or crystallize
your molecules with cold

keep your eyes on the sidewalk,
not paved here,
the puddles from recent rain

the Gulf station
could swallow you like a prairie

you could walk into
that phone booth
and step out between the planets

146 HOTLINE TO THE GULF

   1

A hot wire
into the immense
turquoise
chasm of silence

this slenderest serpent
electrode fanged
excruciatingly
delicately
into my jugular
snaking under my ear
down to the heart's
chambers

it brings me new
perceptions: the world
is not a sphere,
it's a doughnut,
there's a huge
hole at the centre

away down there
are clouds,
a static of voices
remote as angels

   2

Write to me, darling
from the other world.
send me olives.

3

There was this woman
on the radio:
all you had to do
was phone CJOR
and she'd give you
the inside dope
on your loved ones
Passed Beyond.

Turning the dial,
what I heard was
my sister's voice:
What can you tell me
about my little boy?

And I ripped the cord
from the wall,
beat my fists
on the kitchen
counter, crying
against that reaching
more terrible
even than death.

4

A list of things done
with hot wires:
   cauterizing small wounds
   burning off warts
   removing the eyes
   of caged songbirds
   shoving it up the penis
   of prisoners

5

Speak to me
for Gods sake.
There are worse things
than death
though you and I
are not likely
to experience
any of them

6

I could almost climb
that wire down
hand over hand
like a fine chain
dangling
into the cool
abyss

a faint odour
of absence,
windless air,
buzzing
of distant voices
I can't recognize

7

Or that imaginary
ribcage
which sheltered me like
a white picket fence
built with love
expanded,
rushed outward
out of sight:

I'm a red
thing beating
at the centre
of emptiness

only a hot vein
wires me
to the perimeter
straining
to hear syllables
in the hiss of blood

147 SUICIDES

Men on the lips
of high windows
women on bridges
or walking steadily
into water
—no. Think of height
water perhaps
but first air,
plumb trajectories
carving air
our gallant proxies
dropping from
high places
dropping like whole branches
of apples
dropping like meteors
dropping like an invasion
from outer space
worlds in collision
dropping like bombs
on Indo-China
dropping like spent
fireworks (matter
is what falls back
from the luminous high-
arching parabola
of energy: Bergson,
a paraphrase)
sizzling through the air
like jet trails
you can wish on
them as if they were
gifts of nature
the fatal acrobats
falling for
you and me

148 THE DIG

Even where traffic passes
the ancient world has exposed
a root, large and impervious,
humped like a dragon
among the city's conduits.
Look, they say,
who would have thought
the thing so tough,
so secretive?

The Diggers

The bone gloved in clay
shallow perhaps where arches
of feet go over;
they see it as finished
round like a jar;
a shard they see as whole.
Will our bones tell
what we died of?

The diggers
with very gentle fingers
lift up the bones of a woman;
tenderly they take off
her stockings of earth;
they have not such love
for the living
who are not finished
or predicted.

The Bones

The men we see always swift
moving, edged with a running light
like fire; their hands infinitely
potent, working in blood,
commanding the death of animals,
the life of the tribe.

The women we see finished
completed like fat jars,
like oil floating on water:
breasts   bellies   faces
all round and calm.

Their bones should thrash
in the diggers' baskets,
should scream against the light.

Their work bent them
and sex, that soft explosion
miraculous as rain
broke in them over and over,
their bodies thickened like tubers
broke and were remade
again and again crying out
in the heave of breaking
the terrible pleasure
again and again till
they fell away, at last
they became bone.

Even their hands
curved around implements,
pounding-stones, were worshipping
the cock that made them
round and hollow.

But before their falling away
was an anger,
a stone in the mouth.
They would say there is
a great fall like water,
a mask taking shape on air,
a sound coming nearer
like a heavy animal
breaking twigs.

And the flesh stamen
bursting inside them
splayed their bones
apart like spread legs.

*Will our bones tell
sisters, what we died of?
how love broke us
in that helplessly desired
breaking, and men
and children ransacked our flesh,
cracked our innermost bones
to eat the morrow.*

149 CATARACT

First everything turns to rainbows
edges of bronze and blue
doppler colour,
seen through a fine curtain
or the continual cast up
spray from a great fall.

Later the curtain thickens
white fog obscures shapes
hearing grows tense
for the rush and pressure
of blood like a great river
gathering volume
falling among caverns
in the listening skull

rushing toward the gorge
thunder and rub
to the precipice under the ear
to dive like Niagara
into the abyss
the hollow continent
the body

He is locked in
the white space
the mist   and the cataract
of blood he is forced
now to hear   and sways
like earth shaken
by its passage.

150 IN THE SILENCE BETWEEN

In the silence between the
notes of music
something is moving:
an animal
with the eyes of a man
multitudes
clothed in leaves

It is as if huge
migrations take place
between the steps
of music
like round
stones in water:
what flows between is
motion so constant
it seems still

Is it only the heart
beat
suspended
like a planet
in the hollow body
messages of blood
or the sensed arrival
of photons
from the outer
galaxies?

A journey that far
we begin also
advancing
between
progressions of music

the notes make
neuron
paths where we move
between earths
our heads full of leaves
our eyes like
the eyes of humans

Later Uncollected and Unpublished work

1968-1975

151 RIDING PAST

Long street of houses
with lighted roofs
black against

winter sky blue as Venetian glass
with Venus hanging
like a small yellow moon

In the houses people
are cooking food and scolding children
the ones home from work

are hanging their coats up
telephones are ringing
behind the yellow windows

Come, open the doors
yellow rectangles and steam
of meat and potatoes

Stand on the front steps
stare at the sky and wave
Look, we're riding past Venus

152 CHILD, CHILD

Squared sunlight over the desk,
and the real voice of the teacher
nasal and bright as a morning radio
announcer—
wake up and hear the commercial;
next will be
multiplication of fractions.

>Child this is a glittering dark ocean
>alive with un-numbered motions
>orchestrated with motions.
>I know.

Glassed sunlight warm on the hands
and the ruled paper,
and a lock of hair
falling into the eyes,
brushing it back with the hand with
the pencil in it—
first we must find the least common
denominator.

>Child the least motion
>stirs up phosphorescence
>a swimming ripple of light endless.
>child the least motion
>rises a faint foam in the dark of you.
>I know.

The recess orange, peeled and Saran-Wrapped,
in the desk; fibres will cling between the teeth
the juice will leave yellow around the mouth;
afterward there will be a game of
boys chase girls.

        Child it is stranger than sex
        more holy than all the body's
        holiest adventures.
        I know.

The pencil, smooth and hexagonal,
between the fingers, the shuffling of feet,
crisp turning of pages, the neighbour
coughing, the teacher writing with chalk —
turn to page 95 and consider these
problems.

        Child you are a molecule of light
        in a glittering dark ocean
        you are the giant atom
        that begins the universe
        you are swimmer and sea
        in an intricate orchestrated flow
        and the key to its orchestration
        is in you.
        where are you going?
        but I can't turn my eyes upon my eyes
        and know.

153 SKIN OVER POMPEII

That city houses in
my hollow self:
Leviathan I
my skin tents over catacombs
populous as all sub-cellars
of intricate griefs:
stone bone and breath
of those dry mouths
that shaped to love or malice,
moved always pursuing
the sensual words,
the semen of speech;
and eyes that were like wishes
exquisitely skilled
now blind and lucent stone.
Heart and lungs I move
among blunt hands
hurting with beauty
like a sudden horizon of sea,
where light washed through doorways
on the strong decisive faces,
the wide and wishing;
and what was juice
and sumptuous usefulness of flesh
is burned to pure gesture
absolute as stations of a dance
for the mind's oblique lusts
and the gut's sorrows.

154 THE CHINESE GREENGROCERS

They live their days in a fragrance
of white and black grapes
and tomatoes and the fresh
water smell of lettuce.

They know with their hands
and noses the value
of all things grown.
They will make you a bargain price
on overripe cantaloupe.

They wash with clear water
their bunches of carrots
and radishes. They crank out
a canvas awning to shelter them.

Their babies suckle on unsold bananas.
By the age of six
they can all make change
and tell which fruits are ripe.

The grandmothers know only numbers
in English, and the names
of fruits and vegetables.

They open before the supermarkets open,
they are open all day,
they eat with an eye on the door.

They keep sharp eyes
for shoplifting children.
They know every customer's
brand of cigarettes.

After the neighbourhood movies are out
and the drugstores have all closed
they bring in their blueberries
and cabbages and potted flowers.

In the rooms behind the store
they speak in their own language.
Their speech flies around the rooms
like swooping, pecking birds.

Far into the night I believe
they weigh balsa baskets
of plums, count ears of corn
and green peppers.

No matter how they may wash
their fingers, their very pores
are perfumed with green,
and they sleep with parsley and peaches
oranges and onions
and grapes and running water.

155 IT IS THE UNEXPECTED MOTION THAT TAKES US

as when in a fireworks display
a bursting Star blooms downward
in the high air,
the indrawn breath of the crowd
the soft concentrated aah
as the pattern opens outward
like a universe,
then dies.

Or when a dancer's long hair
purls suddenly outward
into a sea fan's shape
waving in air like water
a moment
before it falls.

Or as a twist of words
opens my mind
onto a huge forest
lamped with Rousseau-creatures' eyes
lighting the known way
into the forest
into the most ancient place
a moment
before my eye closes.

156 MOVE ON THE DARK FLOOR

Move on the dark floor
Something in the room tilts open
One is aware of
an opening motion
somewhere attention cannot move

Perhaps like the shift
of shards in a kaleidoscope
a fractured second
hesitation
all constant laws converge
then the new pattern
instantaneous
a visual bell-clap

Perhaps its negative
the moving open in the room
an emptiness of pattern
creating pattern

The floor is like
the long tongue of an iris
or a butterfly's tongue
uncoiled

The room becomes a threat
my throat swallowing
nicotine
a boy's throat
swallowing Acapulco Gold
because they've smoked up
all their matches

when they try to stand
they flop and fumble
laughing like puppies
it's the whole world
full of foggy bushes
that rolls with them
tumbling them like dice

Not within
their awareness the room
the dark floor
where we step locked
outside our brains
and beyond our attention
something perhaps irises
open

Here the dark floor tilts
all ways
there is a corner
for every one
to be tipped into

157 GREEN PANTHERS

They are not exclusively
that youngleaf green
we are all pleased with
(even grass isn't a monotone)
they are also the flame-
green of copper burning,
swamp green, fence-paint
green, emerald's evil gas green.
It is not possible
to determine where one
green blends into another,
even as no one has seen
the creation of green panthers.

Transformations take place
when nobody's looking:
in parking lots,
in urban back lanes
where there are no compost heaps
where every family has
two garbage cans,
inverted air thickens,
takes shape:
material green muscle.

It is possible
they will place heavy paws
on your shoulders, and force you
into the green
niches inside their eyes.
It is possible
they will take M-1 rifles
between their teeth.
It is even possible
they will learn to sing
and form a choir
of perfect harmony.
Their possibilities
are not exclusive.

158 MAGELLAN

1

They are taking me south
over the liquid rim
of the world like that other
they named me for.
Soon now I'll see the clouds
he named, those reefs
which to his European eyes
were cool patches,
mere strangeness where everything
shimmered with strangeness;
the spume of that great light
roiled in his wake
and the new sky lapping
and sliding on water.

I want to see
with these human? eyes.

2

My change comes on me.
Already my lids grow heavy,
the sockets frequently fill
with oil thicker than tears
that runs eventually like tears
but soon will not.

My legs cling together.
My palms adhere
to the curvature
of my thighs.

My skin smooths and toughens.
It is more and more
difficult to wake.

Stewards, attendants,
I'll never see you
as you are, flesh
of my unlikely flesh.

We are becoming
mutually metaphors,
I in my slow chrysalid
sealing mouth eyes fingers,
changing under
a pupa's membrane.

When I am born again
you will be sudden
to me as butterflies,
exotic insects darting
between ticks of sun.
Will we then prize
each other more?

3

You move between love
and that essential solitude
you speak of, but I think you
know solitude only as you know
the sea in a handful of water.

When I am only a beating
yolk, a shadow of purpose
under membrane

smooth as the inside of a mouth,
you will breathe easily
you will comfort each other
you will see the cloud drifts of stars
move across the water;
at times you will believe
you are lonely.

Or you'll stand over me
fascinated, not wishing
to breathe not wishing
to penetrate the skin:
a thing fabulous
as the canals of Mars,
too clouded to reflect
a glance of yours
but you will not be alone.

    4

They knew what they were doing
with me, a nice welding
of science and art—
he was crippled, you know,
before his last voyage:
they believe in symmetry
they knew what they were doing
setting this estranging
watch in me.

Scribbling a molten spectrum
they are quite beyond
my sight, their gnat voices
impossible, except at times
a syllable, my name,

nicks like a feathered dart
at my ears' edges
a breathy scratching
gone before I lift
my eyes, or they place
their so light hands
on me their faces steady
they are trying to get through to me
I see grooves tracing their skin
I see light on their faces
scatter like flicked water:
they flinch

The very world rejects me:
the sun has slipped a cog
gone mad on speed
Mar Pacifica
flutters like a diaphragm
foam whisks the shore
where vegetation jerks
like hunting spiders.

In the spokes of night
I watch the Greater
and the Lesser clouds.
They knew what they were doing:
This twitching frothing planet
stings my nerves
like clouds of insects.
There is no choice now
but to move beyond
the wince and glitter of air,
to steady myself, instrument
of their purpose without choice
for the steady light of Velox Barnardi.

159 SMALL MEMORIALS

1

While I waited for news of your death
small flowering trees
stood cold under the street lights
and Betelgeuse stained
a whole segment of sky bloody.

2

Now that your ashes have been given
to the wind,
times when I breathe
a sudden atom of sourceless laughter
I shall acknowledge you,
my friend.

3

Eating sour cherries by moonlight,
judging the fruit's ripeness
with my fingers only,
I am remembering you.
Perhaps I associate
fruit and garden
with you, triumphant gardener.
Again perhaps
there are ashes in the air.

160 MORALITY PLAY

Watching the light
people exchange
lovers easily pleasantly—
no fuss
no melodrama—
I think god
how sensible
probably fun too

I never lie
with any man but
we grow
tangled inside
each other
a jumbled knot that
fabulists could cut
their tongues on

Is it some
consolation that
I'm a woman
no one has
ever taken
lightly?

161 THE SUN IN NOVEMBER

1. For two days in November
   i lived with the sun:
   that spiky hundreds of colours
   of red and yellow
   medallion blazed
   on my pillow,
   across the table

   at the window
   parting curtains "overcast"
   for the rest of
   the world: the sun
   belonged to me

2. You step through a doorway
   your head is a child's sun mask
   grinning like a cartoon
   of a man grinning.

   How well we have arranged this:
   you take two more steps
   i take two
   and the whole world falls
   perfectly into place

3. Everyone knows the sun
   burns why should i
   be surprised at my flesh
   crisping, curling away?
   why should these black
   bones of arms jutting
   outward startle me?

4. In bed with you
   and Charles Bukowski
   the question is

        will Bukowski make you
        laugh or am i
        going to make you cry
        a little
        more love —
        Close the book.

5.   All day it's the moment
        after we are stupid
        with bliss glazed over
        talking politely
        with strangers not hearing
        our own words
        submerged in our bodies
        under the glaze
        we are baking
        sweet meat baking
        in our own juices

6.   You are two days gone
        it is snowing or raining
        the earth lies to the rain
        or snow as I lay
        to the fall of your kisses
        impermanent as weather
        i write this in my sleep
        wake in a sweat of words
        words only without kisses
        you are two days gone

7.   Until the ferry reached the pass
        i slept, spun like a planet
        around your image
        your gold head
        in all its phases

it's daylight   i wake
from your eyes to blue
water, cloudy sky;
the lighthouse blinks,
islands shake off the night
stretch their hills .
where are you now
how far?

High to my right
a jet plane
breaches sky, strains
at an impossible angle
seeming immobile

grotesque, a saurian
shape, a pterodactyl
the defeat of species
of whole eras
implied in that shape
gross sorrow: my eyelids
weigh like millennia

i thought i slept; the boat
turned, but that plane
sticks, strains like a man
straining toward a woman
clenching desperate absurd
she is crying:
o please yes now *now*

The bodies of men
their pathetic rise
and fall, their splendour
rising upon occasion

      like the sun itself
      their failures ungainly
      as over-evolved animals
      dinosaurs bleat
      anguish when i wake
      again, the plane has
      got it up, vanished
      sheathed in the pale sky

8.   As if i were water
      flowing you split me
      a shoal a tongue of rock
      i must surround
      even the shore
      seems to be moving
      we have to go
      with the tide

9.   *Have your medical card ready.*
      Sit here. You will be called.

      dr. you must understand i am
      not a woman with strong
      reasons for living:
      my children maimed
      as much as cherished
      grow like flowers on
      a geological fault
      my every step shudders
      disaster something
      in a syringe or
      an inhalant can't you
      give me?

      Raise your arms
      over your head. Breathe.

My lover is a catholic
with children in
parochial schools no one
i've loved has been
ultimately any better
for it you must understand
i have reached the point
of weeping in public
a quick injection a pill

Good news: your x-ray shows
spontaneous healing. The hole
in your lung is closing.
There should be no pain.

you understand i have lost
my reflection in windows
even my eyes have turned
pale the hole is
a constant trap i have
never stopped falling
like a ruined house
open to weather it is
snowing or raining

Here is a prescription
for 292s. Avoid anxiety.
Take the sun.

Take the sun.
the sun

take

   the

10. Attending for the usual
friday drink obeying
traffic signals answering
telephones how clumsy
we are constantly stubbing
toes breaking finger
nails walking into
walls it is this
unaccustomed ankle
chain of gravity
the poles have shifted
we are dragged in
huge ellipses catching
at objects hold me
down is love always
a revolution?

11. Something remains
elusive
a cloud curved to
the limbic brain
a weight of photons
matrix
i recognize as you

cellular memory
a steady presence
a caress so subtle
there is no name
for the sense receiving it

i half-turn what...
did you...
a man's head, a corona
burns on my retina.
yes, i say. you.

1. THE FACE

ALWAYS WHEN I wake my first consciousness is of your face, inside me, as it were under my own, as if my features overlay yours. In those first moments the face is stylized, the hair and beard curled like those of statues. Only gradually, as I move, you move too, the face becomes individual.

I do not recall having dreamt of you. I cast back into sleep: a heavy vacancy, neither of us was there.

All faces change minute to minute. Aspects of your face accompany me, changing without waiting for my intention. I do not invent you. The photograph you sent me has an aspect which has occupied me less than others. I must bring it into balance with your other faces.

The face in the photograph is impressive, formidable in fact. The man with that face, I say to myself, can *cope*. That man will always have everything under control. I am perhaps intimidated.

Most often I remember your face close up, foolish-loving, looking much younger. Or with eyes closed kissing, the even tension of shut eyelids, a sheen like wing cases, a detail giving disproportionate pleasure.

But at my first waking I think we are both eyeless, with the brutal dignity of ancient masks. I imagine myself thin and gold, my hands locked at my sides, tongue locked to the roof of my mouth, each hair root locked in its pore. I imagine myself a sarcophagus carried to burial, an image of you static as a photograph locked under my face.

2. THE CLOTHING

You are so much more clothed than I am. Underwear top and bottom, everything tucked in. I could never touch your body by accident. I could never in a casual embrace slide my hand onto skin and body hair. You have to undress first.

And you carry your life like clothing too. It's very becoming, it suits you. Your relationships with the people around you look good, their textures are interesting. You are conscious of origins.

Maybe you have it all worked out: just enough pain and struggle to keep the nerve ends vibrating. Enough disorder to have let you fall in love with me.

I have a longing now to stare at your real face, to question, demand to know you. But you were the one who stared that way into my face. All the time we were together your eyes never left me, I couldn't eat or sleep. And when you asked me to tell you about my life, so that you could picture what I'd
be doing at different hours of the day, I wouldn't answer you.

Listen: every morning I take a razor to the fabric of my life, I cut out a woman shape, I step into it, I go out, I perform, it works. But every morning it has to be done again.

Sometimes I can't get the blade sharp enough, the shape flat enough. I can't manage a protoplasm silhouette one molecule thick.

My shape takes exaggerated depth like those optical-illusion letters they use to advertise religious movies, where the edges go back and back into the page and come together at a point representing infinity. My continuum drags behind me, a rubble of dark and rough and glitter stretching back probably to the point of birth.

Then my whole life seems like the act of birth, as violent and difficult and inescapable. My clothing is bloody membrane and sea water, dragging at my body.

I can't even imagine what you feel like in your turtleneck sweater, checkered pants, tidy underwear.

3. THE MACHINERY

The machinery is, in abstract, like a space wheel in orbit. Stately precise turning into and out of sunlight. If we were separate from it, it would seem lovely. We would breathe in delight seeing it in a movie.

The machine is, of course, a centrifuge. We're locked on its outside walls by the magnetic soles of our feet, the veins branching downward. I think of a glass anatomical model of a man, with an erection.

As if the earth had gone transparent and its gross axis become visible, turning us. Like a drill-core spectrum, a blackened rainbow, the red orange yellow at the centre, further toward the ends roughness, jumble, glisten of oil and coal pools, moving capillaries of water. The ends themselves hard glossy white, ice that never melts. The effortless spin of the thing generating so much brute power.

Sometimes I think I can see you across the curvature of the walls. We might reach out, try to touch.

But the machine holds us motionless. Our muscles flatten, our veins and arteries spread out like maps. We are splayed, pinned down on separate beds, in separate cities.

I'm turning downward into sleep. I will not dream of you. Slowly, slowly, it's turning you toward your morning. You are beginning to remember me.

163 THE BLIND

The blind memorize
terrain
geometry
coffee table   bruises
tall lamps
like spindly animals
teeter and pose
stair risers
nudge your shins
like small dogs

not seeing you
i've gone blind
is a blindness
you have set up
a room furnished
where i live
i know where
the bed is
and the table
tho i've never seen them

nor need to
till absence strikes
like coat hangers
leaping from closets
like a lamp
falling too far
deliberately smashing
windows   ice-thin
blades of glass
everywhere
i can't see

164 DOING IT OVER

Once we've had babies
we can't stop
dreaming them; sound asleep
we grow moon bellies,
relive hospital rituals,
astonish ourselves with
blue-eyed children,
small animated mouths.

The act itself, the orgasm
of delivery
is missed; some things
no dream can recreate.
(But I didn't *want* anaesthetic!
I cry, dead asleep.)

Our arms keep remembering
the cradle shape,
the breasts heavy again,
the milk prickling in
to the glands
(My mother at 64
after the surgeon took
half her stomach
woke up and asked,
Is the baby all right?)

All our lives
swelling and germinating
in our dreams, we may
be more like plants
than we thought:
apple trees can't
forget the seasons

nor can we ever
be done with newness
but make beginnings
over and over again
in the roots of ourselves,
in the dark
between our days.

165 FROM THE GLASS UTERUS

It was a toy I found
marked down Educational
Fun For The Children
Build the transparent woman
with detachable
reproductive system
complete with plastic
embryo

In other years I wouldn't
notice. Now I am
an analogue of glass
I am made toy-size
once again.

It's too late anyway
to care that
that was all in us
they valued.
Their triumphs are too many
to be ordered,
they overlap like sequins
on a mermaid's tail.
I've read and now believe
there are such creatures.

166 MYSTERIES

You are
full of mysterious
valves gears motors
projectors tape recordings:
what has become of
your first love
your grandparents' farm
your inland waters
hairy with weeds and wreckage?

I am also
fitted with odd
switches and sidings:
trains shunt continuously
panting like damaged lungs.
I am wondering how
I got on this old
narrow gauge track
leading away inland
to your last ditch country.

167 SPOOKED

    So I must sleep with a ghost.
        But, Janek, you shouldn't
            have mentioned it —
    it's a nice ghost, really,
    rather a naughty
           young girl — I hear
    her tip-toeing up the stairs
    with her shoes off
    at four in the morning
I smile with polite disbelief.
I am a materialist.

My multi-lingual, consummately
well read friend says:
        I didn't want Pat to know.
        She's sleeping in that room.

Am I still smiling?

        Sometimes I call:
            Come down if you're lonely
            and visit —
    I only hope she hasn't got
    holes for eyes

My eyelids keep standing to attention.
    I am a materialist.
I root among pillows
for a thumb of sleep

Did the stairs creak? Is it
    four o'clock?

168 QUESTION

without ceasing to be me
I can be the bird I see
there on the spray
in every feather he
though in my own way

but where's the guarantee
that I am not some dim
creature in that bird's whim
that makes me be this me
that looks at him?

169 MOON JELLY

The moon jelly rests in your hand
a substance with weight
but without texture or colour;
your life line is clearly visible
through it, every crease of your palm;
it is so frictionless
it can slide off before you know,
then you have to quick
search for the inner ring
like a pattern in crystal,
the only part an eye
can by chance find.

It's the springtide of the moon
full and heavy float the moon jellies
to hands' reach, the glass lace
of their tentacles scarcely moving,
life pure and unexplainable
as quartz or your hand
or the moon driving its flocks
like a fat shepherd.
How do you, really, explain the moon?

1913

44 miles ahead of steel
2 weeks of rain
with no pay and the grade,
supposed to be clay, hits hardpan
and only the blackflies could
drive a man in to the lice
and stench of the bunkhouse
and Antol's brother Stan dies
of flybite, his eyes nose
finally his throat swelled shut
he dies in a frenzy
clawing for breath
and Antol goes to the boss
for his brother's pay
and the boss ticks off
sick time, board on rainy days
overalls towels a pick handle
against $1.10 a day
and it turns out Antol
owes the boss
for his brother's keep
so Antol curses the boss
and jumps work with half
a loaf of bread a tin of tomatoes
a pocketful of matches
a few sentences of English
the line swallows him
and his curses like a fly
and maybe he makes town
the country's too big
for anyone to ask.

171 RANDOM INTERVIEW

1, the fear

the fear is of everything
staying the way it is
and only i changing

the fear is
of everything changing
and i staying the same

the world expanding
branch tunnel cell
more and more
precious and terrible

while i grow only more
fragile and confused

the fear is my own
hands beating
like moths

my eyelids stuttering
light breaking into
meaningless phrases

the fear is of you
patiently elsewhere growing
a blood shape
of all my wishes

2, i am tired

i am tired of pain
i am tired of my own pain
i am tired of
the pain of others

i am tired of lives
unwinding like a roll
of bloody bandage
i shall roll up
the sky, pinch the sun

i go out to the cliff pours
of stars, the tall
volumes of stars

i go down
to the grains of soil
to bacteria
to viruses
to the neat mechanics of molecules

to escape the pain
to escape the pain

3. what i want

what i want is to be blessed
what i want is a cloak of air

the light entering my lungs
my love entering my body
the blessing descending
like the sky
sliding down the spectrum

what i want is to be
aware of the spaces
between atoms, to breathe
continuously the sources of sky,
a veined sail moving,
my love never setting
foot to the dark
anvil of earth

172 THE MUSIC OF WHAT IS

Because the voice singing
raises an instant construct
which, if you are not careful
you will recognize
as the shape of your own blood
against, and competing with, the sky

Because if you let it
music will pace you everywhere,
you will be held to earth
by grave drums and cellos

   drown it out with forks and knives
                 children's cries
                 advertisers

Because a tangible wind
of brass and tenor
can master you as a sail
is mastered, you can be filled,
driven, by passion you would not own

   bury it under hassles and bargains
               bosses and bonuses
           early to bed and
         o reluctantly to rise

The music of what is
scores through the veins
like knowing lightning:
know how we all would
burn with melodrama,
seized by demands of music
to be who we are

but the fear of our full
sized selves sets us burrowing
warm bowers of tablecloths
contracts saturday nights
to be small worried and comfortable
while the terrible royal procession,
the real music, moves past.

173 POSTHUMOUS CHRISTMAS EVE

My father with his Christmas-red vest
and braggart's moustache
is boycotting the party.
It must be Sunday
or Saturday morning
and he's cold and sleepy
fisheyeing his long-haired sons.

Everyone tries
pretending it's Christmas
but the trays of drinks falter
in midair, and the boys
who last year fizzed and glittered
like barely controlled fireworks
are blurry with politeness.

My father's a cold
sulk of absence
in the corners
planted with odourless poinsettias
red as his vest.

174 SERENDIPITY

people I never expected
to make peace with
accept my blessing
through your intercession
and you never know

between you and me nothing
was ever made
complete, but you are
a fact planted in me

like an old tree
at the edge of a clearing
in secure woods

where animals go
to scratch, to shed
against its bark
a season's detritus
of dead skin

moving across the grain
of you, I skin off
years guilts and angers

friends who betrayed me
lovers I betrayed
come young and unscarred
to the touch
of remote love

175 PLANETARIUM POEMS

I

While we've been in this
darkened theatre
years have passed

we have to play them back,
spin the sun backward,
set the sun backward,
set the white and golden
planets swooping
retracing their courses

Look! Three planets
in opposition. when?
March of some future year?

In an afternoon
we could unmake continents;
species could rise
people the earth and die

while we rewind the cosmos,
slower now, steady the
planets, station the sun
at *now.*

2

All day we've shaped skies
now I attempt sleep
my ceiling's grained with stars
windows let in light leaks
compulsively I arrange
spaces. Even with eyes
closed, my head's a dome
with projectors stuck
and will not dim out.

3

Sleeping at last
dreaming, moving in
the assurance of dream
I know that what we
order is reality;
our choice of data
shapes the universe
we are engaged in
pattern recognition

What we wait for
dreaming or awake
is a breath
of total amazement,
tumblers falling   a new
constellation of sense
some thing
some new order we could
never have imagined.

176 LOSING MY HEAD

how can I stop making
myself a victim again
and again I draw back
my hair my neck
someone said is sensitive
as a face I lay
my eloquent neck on your pillow
the worst of it is you
will not cut clean
you will kiss and bruise

you are crossing a lake
in your new sailboat
beating across a pleated
course   the wind is not
steady   you have to work
so hard   lean so far
off balance

how can I fold myself
I am not water
nor even blood
the blood drained from my head
I fell into
the emptiness of my body
I do not believe
I heard your voice
today or ever

now there is no
where dark where the light
does not trouble
the galaxies shine like whales

the light moves
in slow waves
this is a gift
you said take it

I wanted to keep my head
like a precious object
a sorcerer's globe a thing
that has to be draped
and hidden because of the
power in it
I wanted to
send my headless body
into the world of consequence

my blood defeats me
and water
creating ruins in soft stone
blood falling inside my body
makes words of water
a lake
where you are sailing
your happy erratic course
you think of me
only with love

I believe you   why not
I lay my head
beside you   your eyes close
does the light trouble?
the galaxies swim away
at the speed of light
we can never know them

177 WATERSHED

Here the road ends
the mountains ring
with woodpeckers
my parents made a nest
in the long grass,
filled it with easter eggs
for me to find

my mother shrank under		the dog barks
the bedclothes			my father goes out
thunder and lightning		"end of the road"
raved like a maniac		between mountains the air
ringing the telephone		shakes like a bell
over and over			with echoes
the medium is the message

my father took my
mother's nipple,
squirted milk at me:
"See, it doesn't
like you any more.
It belongs to the new baby."

Where the mountain burned
the dead spars rise
from a lace of green
second growth
somewhere a hammer is tapping:
a man, or a woodpecker

178 ELEGY FOR THE SOUTH VALLEY

1

South Valley Dam is silted up,
the slid scree of a whole mountain
is leaning there; some year
when the rains keep
on and on as they do
it will go, and the wind seethe
in the trees,
the cedars toss and toss
and the creek froth
over broken banks
and the work of men
will be all undone

2

We have no centuries
here a few generations
do for antiquity:
logging camps hidden
around the backs of mountains
shacks falling without sound
canyons with timber trestles
rotting to shreds
like broken spiderwebs
straight scars and planks
collapsed on the walls
of improbable mountains
mountains mountains
and the dam that served
a mine that serviced empire
crumbling slowly deep
deep in the bush

for its time
for this country
it's a pyramid
it's Tenochtitlan going back
to the bush and the rain

    3

The gravel pit is eating
South Valley, the way you'd
eat a stalk of asparagus,
end to end, saving the tender
tip for last. It starts
at the highway end
gouging alder and huckleberry
off the creek banks;
dust loosed in the air
precipitates slowly on water
and smooth wet stones.
Each year the tooth marks
go deeper along the valley
higher into the green
overhanging falls and terraces
of water, shearing toward
the head of the south fork
where the dam leans
between time's jaws
waiting for either
the weight of its past
or the hard bite of the future
to bring it down unmade
and original gravel
bury its shards at last.

179 STEREOSCOPY: AN ISLAND

The island was orchards,
dark starry swell of sea
fishes' shimmering ballet
sequined motions of oars.
The island was swung in a saucer of sea
hung in a night of stars—
the soft dark
singing through the orchards;
of perfect sunlight on the Pass,
starfish clutching like hands
under the wharf
gulls crying
arbutus lifting their bodies like poems.

Beneath that soft dream flesh
the sea's bones
shouldering through thin soil,
the pale burnt slopes
of empty pastures,
the signs
: No Smoking in These Woods :
leaves snapping like thin glass underfoot;
here and there houses
given over
to wild rose, nettle, and bird dung
(wasps' nest in a kitchen drawer)
one lavish tree moulting
leaves like yellow transparencies,
black pills of fruit
clotting the ground.
A dead calf beached,
leather and bone salted
dry as salt between tide and tide;
and where the land rears

unprotected
where the soft sand can't cling,
the sea's shape
in the rock,
breaker and crest and foam
of lifted rock.

180 CADA CABEZA ES UN MUNDO

This alone protected
as jewels or ova,
a chalice of smooth bone
a cradle of water:
inside, the strange, gray planet

181 THE ANIMAL PER SE

Bipeds, but that is not important
What matters is
the structure is inside
like an idea
the body is moulded around it
the concept
is similar to art
what matters here is
the tenderness they felt
for their own shapes.

The student should keep in mind
the corollary
of internal structure:
the creatures were unbelievably fragile.

182 SKIN

skin
clown's coat
film that bruises and sags with age
spectrum of odours
continuous death and renewal
universe's limits
incredible fine mesh of danger
most vulnerable prison
(and everyone of us
some times would sell life
for the intimate
touch of skin)
filter and mask and ultimate
test of truth
skin mimics history
dictates its own continent
most divisive and most
unifying theatre
our only meeting place
skin is what learns
and teaches us our lives

183 THEIR HANDS

sinewy pentacles, agile
as things with their own lives
five prongs of bone
knuckled, woven with
loops of muscle
a tough pad of flesh
the play of the bones is
eloquent as faces
the nerves of the finger ends
are knowledgeable,
exercise memory and discretion
the thumbs in their
oiled sockets transform
the organs, infinite shape-makers
stubborn and daring movers—
they'll try anything.

184 HIS EYES EXAGGERATE

his eyes exaggerate everything:
not only the openings.
the orbs themselves are large;
closed, the eyelids are
long and supple.
his eyes establish
empires, demand earth's secrets;
it's comic the way the eyes
deal with difficult objects,
studies which do not yield.
The eyes are also merry,
eat and drink with
the other members,
but are perhaps best
at making choices,
claiming an individual
in a crowd of details;
but their decisions
are never final:
the eyes remain open.

185 HISTORY

Impacted in rock
a lip of calcium
a frill of flesh petrified
a shell valve edge
studded with eyes
ages upon ages
blank cliffhanging
a foot extrudes / a claw
grinds purchase
in time   another age
sifts down dry snow
on double hair
the body's heat won
in clever spaces
revolutions pass and weathers
and a big-jawed childskull
is wreathed with shells
love in abraded stone
a shaman paints his hand's edge
a star on stone
the stone cries
time without voice
life without hands
holding on / holding
on   holding

186 IMAGINE THEIR GENERATIONS

Imagine their generations a vertical frieze
the shapes repetitive as an ocean
the dumb curve of shoulders
bent to their work, their earth.
each figure has one hand cupped
an ambiguous gesture, giving or holding
corn, metal, pollen, or something intricate
and bruisable as a lung; or a coal,
its fragile petals of ash protecting the hand
from the orange-pink heat
at the heart of it.

Feel their shapes in your mind
the smooth humps of shoulders
the angular jack-knife arms
the hands contracted to a calyx
Imagine now time itself grown dense
as coal, impacted
in that one posture.

187 THEIR MYTHOLOGY

They have tales of a god
bruised and humble
born through the body:
it is that passage
through blood and labour
they celebrate —
their origin in darkness
the unimaginable sleep
of the ovum
that passage to wakening,
to ripeness,
plays like cave light
in their wondering:
each life so dearly won.
Could even god forgo
that journey?

188 MOVING SOUTH

This blue star
The crease of dazzle
at zenith
sibilance of light
filtering air
it falls on our eyelids
from inside, it
enters our lungs

moss and willow roots
our hands twined among them
like clever animals
insects rising in flocks
the flocks of birds
diving

we move southward
the silence behind us
widens like a flood
a great cold pour

In our skull's fonts
we carry
huge intricate flowers;
serpents and butterflies
cats with shining pelts

struggle for shape
within our eyes
we shave the insides
of our throats
with razor air
straining for sap smells

we are almost sure now
but keep our habits
formal as hunger
just keep the cupped fire
the breathing coal
under our skins

The animate seed
wind dropped on a precipice
of stony morning
has its imperative: Destroy.
Extend roots. Break rock.

Patience becomes a radula,
a toothed foot
scraping at circumstance.

In the hard wind are you
teeth, a bush of nerves,
a binary clinching:
yes water light growing,
no to the wind's nails
and the rock.

So much depends on
the rock crumbling,
the forced alchemy, humus,
green living rooms built
on the edge of denial.

In your livingroom are you
bent in the wind's hands
grinding against the reef
of the day's death.

189 CONTEXT

Behind the closet door
which is kept firmly closed
after dark
corpses are propped up
waiting to be discovered
ghouls munch their flesh
Dracula sharpens his fangs
Frankenstein's monster
does finger exercises
the closet is infinite in length
goes down to the roots of the earth
werewolves prowl through it
tentacled things hiss
witches couple with horny devils
yes they are all here
eyes, teeth, without faces
tongues spotted with blood
appalling hungers
moans and sick clotted laughter
yes and a parallelogram
of light from another room
lies on the small beds
the children sleep
while the closet door is closed.

190 NEWSREEL

The film is at first confusing:
a spill of running figures
the eye can't recognize
the camera picks out events
a young woman flat
on pavement being clubbed
her face veiled in blood
a young man with his arm
twisted behind him
pushed into a van
men in boots and helmets
faces with mouths stretched moving
the film lurches
out of focus the cameraman
is running a tram
blunders into the scene
a fire hose smashes
all of its windows
a mother picks glass
from a baby's cheek
just off camera a
queue is waiting
to rape a peasant girl
a machine gun fires
directly at the camera
the film splinters white ————
but we do not wake up

191 THINK OF THE WIVES OF MARTYRS

Marie-Rose
thin as a cigarette
wispy and indeterminate as smoke
walks her blind husband
out on Main Street
describes to him store windows
queues at bus stops
remembers him shuddering from traffic
clutching her like a metal child
remembers his tears in private
his rage contained like voltage
in hot wires: her whole life
spitted on that fierce field
her life bound to the axis
of his crucifixion.

192 GREEKS GO BY SINGING

Because it didn't rain
last night in Vancouver
on a quiet street
under the trees the young
Greeks went past singing
the moon and stars
into the sky.
Inside the house he was
saying, I want you to
use me as a friend
I want you to need me.
And under the chestnut
trees seven young men
walked abreast singing
an ancient season.

193 SONG

I think you are a shaggy flower:
where I've touched you
my hands are yellow

194 CONTINUITY

(Masque for two interchangeable players)

unconscious as a weed
as a bird scratching
I prepare my lies
—always astonished
at catching
myself in my own line

*I shall part my
parti-coloured beard
in the middle, in scrolls
like a Red King
the king of Diamonds
king handsome and remote
above power games*

what do you do times
when you have to untangle
your right hand from my hair?
when you start to speak
and my black hair winds
around your tongue,
cutting the membrane?
get up
put your clothes on
go to your office
phone your wife: any messages?

you told me your lips
had turned black,
your whole mouth burned black.

*Those times the sun coughs
hisses at me
I burst my throat
my fingers beating air
I am falling endlessly
to the river:
like hot wax
its glaucous lips await me
You would have me
gyre on a rein of blood
spitted between the sun
and flesh. Draw out
your golden fingernails.*

gulls rise like a cloud of steam
from a garbage dump
I wrestle my life
hooks and bleeding eyes
weights tethers rags
I am frantic to tear
everything down the middle:
the universe is so fragile
stop breathing for a while
and it disappears

*I shall plug my bones,
put on smooth clothing
You will see my face
as a reproduction,
the forehead textureless*

*as plaster,
scarcely a crow's foot
mars the skin
Perhaps I shall speak
only at long intervals.*

yet you will not see me
pinched and bitter
scrawny with age
scrabbling among pebbles
for the stone you laid in me

you would lay me in gold
embroidery, paint
sun on my face
roses between my legs
you would stitch me
with lace of kisses
and see me clothed
in a picture

*Where in this wheeling
aphasia do we meet?
What faces are we wearing?
how do we touch?
for a moment of grace
hands rest together
as though they were fountains
as though they were gardens
a breath's peace only
then we are flying together
helplessly into the sun,
stiff in our formal clothing.*

I am silent now
as if you had taken
language from my mouth.
broken like hands, my parts
of speech lie tangled at your lips.
a stone lies on my tongue.
you have put silence
in me like an egg.
My love, your innocence
your good luck, leave me speechless
even when you mumble
to me dazed blessings
my own mouth impedes.

NOTES ON THE POEMS

Early Unpublished and Uncollected Work (1961–1967)

1 One of the contest poems published in the *Alberta Poetry Yearbook* (1961) under PL's previous marital name, "Patricia Domphousse."

2 "A Moral Tale" first appeared in an obscure, undated anti-war pamphlet entitled *Poems for Life*.

4 The typescript of this unpublished poem is dated May 7, 1962.

6-8; Early examples of the poems which appeared in the Vancouver
11 Poetry Society's magazine, *Full Tide*, between 1962–64.

12 "Choice" originally appeared in *A Biannual of Poetry*, Winter 1965.

13 "Division" appeared with "Before the Wreckers Come" (#15) in *Canadian Poetry*, Spring 1965.

14 "The Squatter"'s references to "a confiscated Japshack" and "that terrible abrupt / exodus" refer to the expulsion of Japanese-Canadian citizens from the coastal region, including the Gulf Islands, during World War II. PL would continue to write of the "encroaching" signs of human habitation on such sanctuaries as Mayne Island in later works such as "Private Ownership" (#105) and "Stereoscopy: An Island" (#179).

16 PL suffered from a skin condition which was aggravated by sun and heat; in later years, she was also prescribed tranquilizers which sometimes induced soporific effects.

18 "[R]emember the nuremburg laws": as an example of institutionalized racism, PL invokes 1935 pre-war Germany, when the Nazis passed anti-Jewish legislation preventing German Jews from marrying or having sexual relations with German citizens. "Lydia's Children" first appeared in *Prism International*, Summer 1965.

26 "A Water Clock" first appeared, along with "With Ferns in a Bucket" (#38) in *The Fiddlehead*, 1966.

27 "History Lessons" first appeared in *The Fiddlehead*, Summer 1967.

28 PL befriended Milton Acorn shortly after her move to Vancouver in 1963; according to her friend, Lorraine Vernon, Acorn is also the touchstone for "Mr. Happyman is Coming" (#101). But the friendship would end in 1974, when, as PL confessed to Fred

Cogswell in a letter dated February 25, 1974, Acorn had "somehow fantasized that relationship into something it never was ... with the result that I really don't want to see him again."

This Difficult Flowring (1968)

29 Earlier manuscript typescript draft titled "Love is to Go On Living with Each Other."

31 "Le Roy S'Avisera": *i.e.*, "the king will think it over"; an obsolete phrase from the history of parliamentary debate.

35 Manuscript typescript dated May 7, 1962.

41 Manuscript version includes semi-colon after line "down a clef into the sea."

42 First published in *West Coast Seen*, eds. Jim Brown and David Phillips (Vancouver: Talon, 1968), along with "Notes From a Far Suburb" (#46), "Visit to Olympus" (#65), and "Child, Child" (#152).

44 Manuscript version places colon rather than comma after line "a conditional pass."

45 First published in *Edge*, Spring 1967

49 Titled after the 1897 painting by Henri Rousseau, a painter of abiding interest to PL.

50 The version published in *This Difficult Flowring* omits a final, third part which appeared in the poem's previously published form in *Talon: Special Issue for the UBC Festival of the Arts*, 1968:

iii   Amphibia dances,
glides through all elements,
porpoise-sports,
balances
need and pleasure,
synthesis,
O delicate ease and skill!
But is a dream,
is symbol of tree
or rainbow bridge,
the gloried swimming
dance of leaf and light
we dream,
but may have cast
with wrinkled reptile-skins
deep in the past.

52 Published first in *Cyclic*, Autumn 1965.

54 As with "flowring," the variant spelling of "granchildren" is deliberate.

56 Manuscript version includes stanza breaks after the line "and even brief touches / of real bodies," in the poem's second part for the "single voice," and after the line, "And maybe those clenched five-petalled palms / will uncurl partly, / enough for touch," in the poem's final sequence.

The Age of the Bird (1972)

57 Based in part on the death of Marxist guerrilla leader Che Guevara, *The Age of the Bird* is the first major indication of PL's interest in Latin American politics, but the poem also anticipates her concerns with evolutionary time and prehistorical origins. In its original publication form as part of Blackfish Press' broadside series, "Regard to Neruda" (#88) was also appended to the long poem as part of the unbound chapbook.

From Infinite Mirror Trip (1974)

58 A logical progression from such earlier experimental works as "The Insider (A Poem For Voices)," *Infinite Mirror Trip* reflects PL's imaginative engagement with the realm of the theoretical sciences, notably astrophysics and evolutionary cosmology. In the early 1970s, the phenomenon of "black holes" and theories of the "big bang" origin of the galaxy were just beginning to circulate in mainstream media. For more on the background of this performance production, see the Introduction of this book.

Milk Stone (1974)

60 "Woman On/Against Snow," written around 1970 and first published in *White Pelican*, Autumn 1971, draws on a complex web of ethnographic and Inuit mythological sources to re-tell the story of Nuliajuk and the lone "Eskimo" woman in counterpoint to the white speaker's observing "eye"/I. For a full discussion of sources, background, and the poem's significance in the context of PL's evolving poetics, see Jean Mallison, "Woman On/Against Snow: A Poem and its Sources," *Essays on Canadian Writing* 32 (1986): 7–48 and Christine Wiesenthal,

The Half-Lives of Pat Lowther (Toronto: UTP, 2005): 256–68. Earlier versions of "Woman On/Against Snow" conclude with an alternate stanza that indicates PL's tightening of the poem during its final revisions: "and her hands stiffen working/ the human statement/ and her breath will go out/ on a song."

62 PL conceptualized "In the Continent Behind My Eyes" as "the core poem sequence" of *Milk Stone*. "Largely concerned with the Ice Age," in her words, this long poem was crafted around two shorter "Ice Age" segments which appear as the italicized portion of the sixth section of Part I and the first italicized portion of the second section of Part III.

The second and final italicized portion of the Part III was published as separate, short poem, "Killing the Bear" in *Forty Women Poets of Canada*, eds. Dorothy Livesay and Seymour Mayne (Montreal: Ingluvin, 1971), along with other *Milk Stone* poems, "Woman" (#73), "TV" (#93), and "Mr. Happyman is Coming" (#101). "Reread my first boc": i.e., "book." In keeping with the poem's archaic theme, PL uses one of the obsolete "first" forms of the Old English word, boc, from Teutonic roots.

63 Earlier published in *Blackfish*, Fall 1971, along with the other *Milk Stone* poems, "Now" (#71), "Woman" (#73), "Psyche" (#76), "At the Last Judgement We Shall All be Trees" (#70), "Arctic Carving" (#66), "Moonwalk Summer" (#89), "To Capture Proteus" (#97), "The Electric Boy" (#99), "Journey of the Magi" (#100), and, finally, "Coast Range" (#113), the re-publication of which PL routed to the later *A Stone Diary*.

64 First published in *The Fiddlehead*, Spring 1972, along with "Demons" (#77), "Toward a Pragmatic Psychology" (#92), and "The Last Room" (#74).

67 First published in *The Merry Devil of Edmonton*, Fall 1969.

68 First published, along with "Wanting" (#75), in *Intrepid: Poetry of Canada*, Summer/Fall 1969.

72 Earlier manuscript typescript draft was titled "Beginning" and slated for inclusion in a preliminary "Table of Contents" list for *This Difficult Flowring*.

78 First published in *Mountain Moving Day*, ed. Elaine Gill, 1973, along with "The Earth Sings Mi-Fa-Mi" (#111) and "Morality Play" (#160).

82 First published in *The Fiddlehead*, Winter 1970, along with "The Chinese Greengrocers" (#154).

83 First published in *Quarry*, Summer 1974, along with "Wrestling" (#122).

86 PL wrote this tribute poem after reading Livesay's *The Unquiet Bed*, and an unspecified "book on gardening, some of which is plagiarized in the poem" (letter, 23 April, 1969). It was first published in *Quarry*, Fall 1969 under the title "Growing Seasons."

87 PL's interest in Bly was as a political poet: during the sixties and seventies, Bly was influential as an editor who introduced a number of important European and South American poets, Neruda included, to North American audiences. He was also a leading figure of opposition to the Vietnam War, having co-founded the American Writers Against Viet Nam in 1966. "Laid in some dreamy Edna": an allusion to the "cell-small" "frontier" town of Edna, Texas?

A Stone Diary

102 First published in the *University of Windsor Review*, fall,
-103 1973.

104 First published in *Blackfish*, Winter/Spring 1972–73, along with "Anemones" (#116).

105 The Gulf Islands, and especially Mayne Island, held a special significance for PL as a family retreat where her relatives owned property (cf also for example, "Song," [#115]). During the sixties and seventies, demand for recreational property increased exponentially, leading to the subdivision on the major islands, and outright purchase of many of the smaller islands in the area.

106 "Annie McCain": PL's maternal grandmother, *née* Wilks, b. 1876–d. 1949. In an earlier draft, the penultimate line of stanza three read "useless at woman things." "Inheritance" was first published in *Event* 2/3, 1971–73, along with "City Slide/2" (#137).

108 PL began writing "The Pit," as it was originally titled, right around the time of the Chilean *coup*, in late September 1973. The events alluded to include the overthrow of democratically elected President Allende by the US-backed *junta* military force, and the incarceration (if not torture) of hundreds of political prisoners. In a letter to Eugene McNamara, dated December 31, 1973, PL noted: "I'm playing the Messiah and a scratchy old record of Columbus Boys Choir singing Bach's

Easter Cantata. Slowly writing a poem about Chileans imprisoned in disused nitrate mines, and it seems to be mixed up with this kind of music. Counterpoint, maybe." For a fuller discussion of the poem's sources and techniques, see Wiesenthal, *The Half-Lives of Pat Lowther*, Toronto: University of Toronto Press, 2005: 279–89.

109 Leonard George: Salish native leader, born and raised in North Vancouver, member of the Tsleil-Wantuth Nation, and youngest son of Chief Dan George (b. 1899–d.1981).

110 Furry Creek, near Squamish, BC, was an area well known by Roy Lowther, and served as a bucolic retreat from the city for PL and Roy in early days of their marriage. The earliest drafts of "Furry Creek," as it was first titled, date from this period. The finalized version was first published in *Inscape*, Spring 1974, along with "Intersection" (#145). For a fuller discussion see Wiesenthal, *The Half-Lives of Pat Lowther*, Toronto: University of Toronto Press, 2005: 370–75 and Keith Harrison, "Notes on 'Notes from Furry Creek,'" *Canadian Literature* 155 (1997): 39–48.

111 "January 1973": Perhaps to mark the signing of the Paris Peace Accords, "Ending the War and Restoring Peace in Vietnam," 27 January, 1973.

113 The North Shore Mountains "just north" of PL's childhood home in North Vancouver. "They don't speak Rosicrucian": i.e., an esoteric language, pertaining to the seventeenth-century spiritual movement. For a fuller discussion of the poem's engagement of topical environmental and political issues, see Wiesenthal, *The Half-Lives of Pat Lowther*, Toronto: University of Toronto Press, 2005: 358–63.

114 First published along with "Hotline to the Gulf" (#146) in *Lakehead University Review*, Summer 1974.

116 –120 All written between 1972–74, a period during which PL joked, "I'm having a tremendous love affair with invertebrates" (audio tape recording, possession of Beth Lowther). "Slugs" was first published in *West Coast Review*, Fall 1973; "Octopus," "Hermit Crabs," and "Craneflies in Their Season" were first published, along with "Last Letter to Pablo" (#129), "The Blind" (#163), and "Doing It Over" (#164) in *Woman's Eye: Twelve BC Poets*, ed. Dorothy Livesay (Vancouver: AIR, 1974). For a fuller discussion of the "beast poems" in the context of

PL's poetics, see Wiesenthal, *The Half-Lives of Pat Lowther*, Toronto: University of Toronto Press, 2005: 375–78.

121 First published, with "Posthumous Christmas Eve" (#173) and "Serendipity" (#174) in *Event* 3, 1975.

124 First published with "Suicides" (#147) and "It Happens Every Day" (#143) in *The Fiddlehead*, Summer 1973.

125 Both prior to and after Neruda's death in 1973, PL worked on
-129 this sequence of 'letters' 'to' Neruda. On the Chilean poet/stateman's significance for PL and her poetic development, see Wiesenthal, *The Half-Lives of Pat Lowther*, Toronto: University of Toronto Press, 2005: 270–81, and Mervyn Nicholson, "Lowther, Neruda and the Secret Wisdom of Food," *Essays on Canadian Writing* 78 (2003): 220–42. "Anniversary Letter to Pablo" was previously published in the international tribute anthology, *For Neruda, For Chile*, ed. Walter Lowenfels (Boston: Beacon Press, 1975), and prior to that, appeared in a small American quarterly, *Inscape*, in 1974. But the poem's date of composition is less certain than that of the other Neruda poems, which PL wrote during 1972, and later followed up, after Neruda's death, with "The Last Letter"—a work she described as "very definitely a post-script to [the] earlier group of 'Letters'" (letter to Dorothy Livesay, January 9, 1974). On the ambiguities of the placement of "Anniversary Letter to Pablo" in the wider sequence, see Wiesenthal, *The Half-Lives of Pat Lowther*, Toronto: University of Toronto Press, 2005: 444.

130 First published in *Mainline*, Spring 1973.

134 This poem was inspired, PL explained, by a friend who was the victim of random violence, murdered while on vacation in Hawaii: "She just woke while her room was being robbed, and was [killed]. But I thought, anyone who stabbed somebody that many times, there must have been some real anger there."

136 "City Slide/4" (#139), omitted from Oxford University Press'
-142 edition, is here restored in this series; see Introduction.

148 In its original publication in *The Antigonish Review*, Winter 1974, the poem is formatted to begin mid-way down the page. For a fuller discussion of PL's interest in earth science and archaeology, and for an analysis of the poem's structure, see Wiesenthal, *The Half-Lives of Pat Lowther*, Toronto: University of Toronto Press, 2005: 378–83.

Later Unpublished and Uncollected Work (1968–75)

153 Anticipating later poems such as "The Dig," "Skin Over Pompeii" was first published in *West Coast Review*, Fall 1969.

154 In addition to its original publication in *The Fiddlehead* (see note to poem #83), "The Chinese Greengrocers" was re-printed in *Best Poems of 1970: Borestone Mountain Poetry Awards: A Compilation of Original Poetry Published in Magazines of the English-Speaking World in 1970* (Palo Alto, Pacific Books, 1971).

155 Gauging from notebook evidence, in which it appears after a draft of "Moonwalk Summer" dated "July 23, 1969," "It Is the Unexpected Motion that takes Us" was composed circa 1969–1970.

156 First published in *Black Moss*, Winter 1972, and re-printed in *Printed Matter: An Anthology of Black Moss*, 1973, "Move on a Dark Floor" reflects PL's typical concerns with forms of structural instability also evident in such domestic poems as "In the Complicated Airflow" (#41) and "Toward a Pragmatic Psychology" (#92).

157 The title inevitably evokes the nationalist Black Power organization of the mid-sixties, the Black Panthers. A slightly different version of "Green Panthers" was first published in *Mainline*, Fall 1972, with the final lines, "*These* possibilities / are not exclusive."

158 Ferdinand Magellan (b. ca. 1480–d. 1521), Portuguese explorer and astronomer, whose successful circumnavigation of the globe provided the first positive proof of the Earth's rotundity, and gave a more accurate idea of the distribution of land masses and water. Both the Straits of Magellan, south of mainland Chile, and the Magellanic Clouds of the Southern Hemisphere are named after him. "Mar Pacifica": Magellan named the Pacific ocean. "Velox Barnardi": or "Barnard's Star," one of the sun's nearest neighbours, named after astronomer E.E. Barnard in 1916.

161 Written in late 1973, after a brief rendezvous on Vancouver Island with her long-distance lover, Eugene McNamara. Thematic similarities to the autobiographically inflected "Sun in November" may be detected in "Continuity" (#194) which PL may, in fact, have begun around the same time (see Introduction). "Charles Bukowski": the prolific and colourful

American poet whom PL met at least once at a reading in southern Ontario. "Take the sun. / the sun // take// the//": an apparent echo of the conclusion to Henrik Ibsen's *Ghosts: A Domestic Drama in Three Acts* (1881).

162 "The Face" first appeared in *Prism International*, Fall 1974, just as PL was completing work on the multi-media production of *Infinite Mirror Trip* at the MacMillan Planetarium. In that show, PL had made use of the image of a wheel in the form of Leonardo da Vinci's "Universal Man" or "Vitruvian Man," as one of the production's special effects. As marginal notes on an earlier draft of "The Face" suggest, however, her reference in Part 3, "The Machinery" to "a space wheel in orbit" drew specifically on the image of the wheel-shaped space station and Ferris-wheel effects from Stanley Kubrick's 1968 sci-fi classic, *2001: A Space Odyssey*. The film's treatment of the themes of evolution, technology, and artificial intelligence held obvious interest for PL.

165 While the title "*from* The Glass Uterus" suggests an excerpt from a longer work, PL seems to have settled on this text as the finalized poem. She abandoned an earlier notebook draft which included a brief second section and an unfinished third part.

167 -168 The date of composition and placement of these two poems is speculative, guided mainly by the notebook in which the text appears, in the case of "Spooked" (#167). "Question" (#168) is an even more ambiguous case, since the poem appears to exist only as a single scrap of loose-leaf typescript among PL's papers. While its overt rhyme scheme and stanza structure recall PL's earlier formalist verse, a later date for the poem's composition is suggested by the fact that this text was among the material collected by police as evidence in the trial against Roy Lowther after PL's death, as was the case only with her recent work. Furthermore, despite its more regular form, "Question" reflects the riddling quality of much of PL's mature work, probing the same paradoxes of identity as, for example, such poems as "I.D." (#130) and "Reflecting Sunglasses" (#135) from *A Stone Diary*.

173 Although not published until 1975 (see note to poem #121), "Posthumous Christmas Eve" was written in 1970, shortly after the death of PL's father, Arthur Tinmouth Jr. (b.1908–d.1970).

175 -176 First published in *A Lake Superior Journal*, Winter/Spring 1975.

177 "Here the road ends": the poem's setting evokes PL's first childhood home, beyond the outermost fringes of the municipality of North Vancouver, at the Lynn Creek water intake. "Watershed" was first published in *Event*, Fall 1975.

178 A companion poem to "Notes From Furry Creek" in many respects, "Elegy for the South Valley" was not included in PL's typescript for *A Stone Diary*, but published first instead in Gary Geddes' *Skookum Wawa: Writings of the Canadian Northwest* (Toronto: OUP, 1975). "It's Tenochtitlan": place name of the seat of the Mesoamerican empire (1325–1521 AD), the ruins of which are in Mexico City. For further discussion, see Wiesenthal, *The Half-Lives of Pat Lowther*, Toronto: University of Toronto Press, 372–75.

179 Like "Notes from Furry Creek," "Stereoscopy: An Island" appears to have had a long evolution, spanning multiple drafts over many years (see Introduction). This version, from a typescript draft, is a considerably tighter revision of the earliest drafts of "The Island," and appears to date circa 1974–75 (?). "Sunlight on the Pass": Active Pass, the body of water between Mayne Island and Galiano Island to its north west.

180 -194 These final fifteen poems represent the contents of PL's "Time Capsule" typescript, the project she mentioned as in-progress shortly before her death (see Introduction). In the untitled notebook version, the poems appear in the following order: "Moving South" (an incomplete draft), "Continuity," "Newsreel," "Context," "Skin," "The Animal Per Se," "Cada Cabeza es un Mundo," "Their Hands," "History," "Think of the Wives of Martyrs," "His Eyes Exaggerate," "Their Mythology," and "Imagine Their Generations." "Song" and "Greeks go by Singing" appear in the typescript manuscript entitled "from Time Capsule," but not in the notebook containing the other "Time Capsule" poems. The arrangement here is necessarily provisional, based on PL's verbal description of the project during a reading on Prince Edward Island in the summer of 1975. **180:** Cada Cabeza es un Mundo": the title translates as "each mind is a world," or "every mind is its own world." **188:** The notebook version of "Moving South" ends after the sixth stanza. The poem's last five stanzas (from "[t]he animate seed" on) also exist among PL's papers as a separate, untitled typescript, suggesting that she may have amalgamated the two parts at a later stage.

INDEX OF PREVIOUSLY UNPUBLISHED POEMS

After a Day Canoeing, 47
Ballad of a Carefully Bolstered Illusion, 28
City Slide / 4, 233
Context, 312
Continuity, 315
Creek Delta, 47
Echo, 29
Greeks Go by Singing, 314
Haiku, 31
His Eyes Exaggerate, 306
History, 307
Infinite Mirror Trip, 103
Music of What Is, The, 290
Newsreel, 313
Question, 284
Rocks in Copper-Bearing Water, 48
School Children in Spring, 29
Skin, 304
Song, 315
Split Rock, 49
Spooked, 283
Squatter, The, 37
Stereoscopy: An Island, 301
Summer Sickness, 42
Think of the Wives of Martyrs, 314
To Milton Acorn, 53

INDEX OF PREVIOUSLY UNCOLLECTED POEMS

After Rain, 30
Blind, The, 278
Child, Child, 254
Division, 36
Face, The, 275
Losing My Head, 296
Lydia's Children, 44
Moral Tale, A, 28
Morality Play, 268
Move on the Dark Floor, 260
Pastorale, 27
Skin Over Pompeii, 256
Watershed, 298

INDEX OF POEM TITLES

100, 227
1913, 286
After a Day Canoeing, 47
After Rain, 30
Age of the Bird, The, 97
Amphibia, 78
Anemones, 209
Angel, 75
Animals Per Se, The, 303
Anniversary Letter to Pablo, 217
Arctic Carving, 133
'At the Last Judgement We Shall All Be Trees', 136
Baby You Tell Me, 67
Ballad of a Carefully Bolstered Illusion, 28
Before the Wreckers Come, 40
Belly Thoughts, 61
Beth, 43
Blind, The, 278
Birdsong, 31
Birthdays, 214
Burning Iris I, 147
Burning Iris II, 148
Burning Iris III, 149
Cada Cabeza es un Mundo, 302
Cataract, 249
Chacabuco, the Pit, 191
Chant of Hands, A, 85
Child, Child, 254
Chinese Greengrocers, The, 257
Choice, 34
City Slide / 1, 230
City Slide / 2, 231
City Slide / 3, 232
City Slide / 4, 233
City Slide / 5, 234

City Slide / 6, 234
City Slide / 7, 235
Coast Range, 205
Complicated Airflow, The, 65
Context, 312
Continuity, 315
Craneflies in Their Season, 210
Creek Delta, 47
Damn Doom, 55
Dark, 207
Demons, 145
Dig, The, 246
Diviners, 60
Division, 36
Doing It Over, 279
Early Winters, 186
Earth Sings Mi-Fa-Mi, The, 203
Echo, 29
Egg of Death, The, 81
Elegy for the South Valley, 299
Face, 204
Face, The, 275
Five Diptychs
    The Burnings, 169
    To Capture Proteus, 170
    The Falconer, 172
    The Electric Boy, 176
    Journey of the Magi, 178
For Robert Bly Saying Poems, 159
For Selected Friends, 154
From The Glass Uterus, 281
Greeks Go by Singing, 314
Green Panthers, 262
Greetings from the Incredible Shrinking Woman, 216
Growing the Seasons, 157
Haiku, 31

Haunting, 164
Hermit Crabs, 211
His Eyes Exaggerate, 306
History, 307
History Lessons, 52
Hotline to the Gulf, 241
How Can I Begin, 113
I.D., 224
I Lift to the Notes, 32
Imagine Their Generations, 308
Infinite Mirror Trip, 103
In Praise of Youth, 84
In the Continent Behind My Eyes, 118
In the Silence Between, 250
Inheritance, 189
Insider, The (A Poem for Voices), 88
Intersection, 238
Ion, 50
It Happens Every Day, 236
It Is the Unexpected Motion that Takes Us, 259
Jesus Child, 167
Killer Whale, 80
Kitchen Murder, 237
Last Letter to Pablo, 221
Last Room, The, 142
Le Roy S'Avisera, 57
Leaning from City Window, 74
Leonard George, and, Later, a Rock Band, 199
Letter to Pablo 2, 218
Letter to Pablo 3, 219
Letter to Pablo 4, 220
Letter to the Majority, 168
Levitation, 226
Losing My Head, 296

Lydia's Children, 44
Magellan, 263
May Chant, 56
Midterm Exam, 68
Moon Jelly, 285
Moonwalk Summer, 162
Moral Tale, A, 28
Morality Play, 268
Move on the Dark Floor, 260
Moving South, 310
Mr. Happyman is Coming, 180
Music of What Is, The, 290
Mysteries, 282
Neither Did Trees Ringing, 155
Newsreel, 313
Nightmare, 190
Notes from a Far Suburb, 72
Notes from Furry Creek, 201
Now, 137
Octopus, 210
On Reading a Poem Written in Adolescence, 60
On the Bridges, 30
Origin of the Universe, The, 130
Pastorale, 27
Patience, 156
Penelopes, 150
Periodicity, 135
Piercing, The, 146
Planetarium Poems, 294
Poetry, 33
Posthumous Christmas Eve, 292
Private Ownership, 188
Prometheus, 58
Psyche, 144
Question, 284
Random Interview, 287

Reflecting Sunglasses, 229
Regard to Neruda, 161
Remembering How, 59
Riding Past, 253
Rocks in Copper-Bearing Water, 48
Rumours of War, 185
Salaal, 49
Salt Wafers, 46
School Children in Spring, 29
Serendipity, 293
Seven Purgative Poems, 70
Skin, 304
Skin Over Pompeii, 256
Sleeping Gypsy, The, 77
Slugs, 212
Small Memorials, 267
Solstices, 163
Song, 208
Song, 315
Spin Spun, 63
Spitball, 225
Split Rock, 49
Spooked, 283
Squatter, The, 37
Stereoscopy: An Island, 301
Stone Deaf, 134
Stone Diary, A, 183
String-Figure Man Outside the Door, 117
Suicides, 245
Summer Sickness, 42
Sun in November, The, 269
Suspended, 213
Their Hands, 305
Their Mythology, 309
Then, 61
There Were Giants in the Earth, 131

Think of the Wives of Martyrs, 314
Thinner Than, 64
To a Woman Who Died of 34 Stab Wounds, 228
To Milton Acorn, 53
Touch Home, 138
Toward a Pragmatic Psychology, 165
TV, 166
Two Babies in Two Years, 66
Two, Sleeping, 82
Vision, 134
Visit to Olympus, 132
Wanting, 143
Water Clock, A, 51
Watershed, 298
With Ferns in a Bucket, 62
Woman, 139
Woman On/Against Snow, 114
Wrestling, 213

PAT LOWTHER was born in North Vancouver in 1935. In addition to four children, she produced three volumes of poetry, the last of which, *A Stone Diary,* was published posthumously in 1977. Her other works included *The Age of the Bird,* an unbound broadsheet folio, and *Infinite Mirror Trip: A Multimedia Experience of the Universe,* an experimental performance piece originally staged in Vancouver's MacMillan Planetarium. Pat Lowther's contributions to Canadian literature and culture extended to her service as a dedicated arts administrator and a social activist.

CHRISTINE WIESENTHAL is the critically acclaimed author of *The Half-Lives of Pat Lowther,* a biography shortlisted for the 2006 Governor General's Literary Award for Nonfiction. She has published numerous works of nonfiction and poetry, including *Instruments of Surrender,* a collection shortlisted for the Stephan G. Stephannson and the Gerald Lampert awards in 2001 and 2002. She currently lives in Edmonton.

....

¶ A NOTE ON THE TYPE: The text face is Trump Mediäval designed by Georg Trump and first issued in 1954. The display face is the anachronistic Futura, a geometric sans serif designed by Paul Renner in 1924–26. The typewritten letters that appear on the section title pages and the typographic ornaments in "The Age of the Bird" are scans from Pat Lowther's original manuscripts.